Geopolitical U
Eastern Eu

Background and significanc ... the continent

A German view

to Heather

by Stefan Korte

Original:
Geopolitische Umwälzungsprozesse in Osteuropa
Hintergründe und Bedeutung für den Kontinent
Eine deutsche Sicht

Title:
Geopolitical Upheaval in Eastern Europe
Background and significance for the continent
A German view

Author: Stefan Korte
Editor: Gregory Lauder-Frost

ISBN 978-82-93925-23-1

Cover and back illustration: Stefan Korte

Layout: Richard Krogstad

LEGATUM PUBLISHING AS
www.legatum-publishing.com

Acknowledgements

I would like to express my sincere thanks to all those involved in the development and production of this book. Furthermore, I would like to thank the publisher, Legatum Puplishing AS, for their interest and willingness to publish this book.

Because of their special contribution to the creation of this book, in the form of numerous discussions on the topics and the painstaking work of editing, I would like to thank in particular,

Kai Mader,
Gregory Lauder-Frost,
Algis Avizienis,
Daniela Mauser

Last but not least, I would like to thank my dear mother,

Regina Korte,

for all her help, consideration and understanding in the last few months, which were marked by much hardship and little time for the family. Thank you for being there for me!

Remark for the English edition

No equivalent in English could be found for some footnotes in the book. I apologise for this, but the press has different views from country to country on what should and should not be reported. I have taken the liberty of quoting the German version. Fortunately, today, it is relatively easy to translate the texts into English. I apologise for the inconvenience.

Table of contents

Foreword

The Superpowers Eclipse the European Nation-States

Despite the intense political rivalry among the European Great Powers, Europe in the 19th century managed to avoid the widespread destruction of the 20th century's two World Wars. The 19th century after the end of the Napoleonic Wars was a time of relative peace compared to the 20th century. As Henry Kissinger noted in his "A World Restored: Metternich, Castlereagh and the Problems of Peace, 1812-22," European armed clashes of that century tended to be of local significance and short duration. The outcomes did not represent total defeat for the losing side.

It was only later when rivalry among European states was subsumed into global competition involving continental powers, such as Russia and the US, that military conflicts assumed a total aspect. Although recurring tension and periodic clashes characterized the period after the Congress of Vienna, the major European nations never seriously contemplated the total elimination of their strongest rivals. It was tacitly accepted that competition should remain at the margins, observed Kissinger. The former US Secretary of State did not expand on this intriguing observation, beyond stating that the major players of that time were interested in maintaining stability. We might elaborate on this idea. It could very well be that the European Powers restrained themselves in their pursuit of power because they felt a common responsibility for the continuation of European culture and civilization.

By contrast, during World War II, the Soviet Union and the US were not as inhibited in their aspirations, possibly because their ties to European culture were more tenuous. Indeed, their goals were of a universal stamp, and they regarded the Western European theatre of war as only one of several. World War II represented a fight to the death between opposing ideologies and civilizations. Moreover, this war was incredibly devastating because the new continental powers could employ previously unimagined quantities of human and economic resources for war making. At the end of World War II, wide swathes of Europe, with its bombed-out cities, resembled the surface of the moon.

The essential difference between World War II and earlier European armed conflicts was that two non-European powers (the US and the USSR) emerged as the victors. Beginning in 1945, these two enormously powerful continental states proceeded to entrench their enormous influence in the political, economic and cultural spheres of European life. The US and the USSR, both organized on the basis of universal principles, aimed to extend their sway not only over Europe but also over the rest of the world. Europe had become just one of a number of geographic regions into which the superpowers projected their power and competed for influence. Europe was no longer the center radiating power and influence over the four corners of the earth. Instead, its status declined to being a playground (a very important one, to be sure) in which the US and USSR vied for influence.

Although during the Cold War the US and USSR appeared to be implacable enemies ,these two global powers nevertheless had one thing in common – both sought the re-education of Europeans in the spirit of internationalism. Universal doctrines are essential ideological weapons for powers which harbor global ambitions. In striving for global dominance, the superpowers projected worldviews tailored for everyone, without regard to affiliations of race, nationality or religion.

The Soviets labored indefatigably in Eastern Europe, using a combination of murder, terror, mass deportations, comprehensive indoctrination and material inducements. In the West the Americans threw their colossal economic weight behind the project for a united Europe, drawing Western European economies into the global trading system that later gave rise to a standardized consumer culture. Caught in the vise of these two continental giants, European political elites in essence ceased their earlier efforts to integrate the individual in national communities. Urged on by their superpower overseer, West European elites turned their attention to the propagation of internationalist and individualistic values, the development of a consumer society and the competition for foreign markets.

The US nuclear umbrella and military presence in Europe relieved the West Europeans of much of the economic burden of protecting themselves against the threat in the East. This released huge reserves of national wealth for the post-war prosperity boom. As a result, the individual was free to indulge himself, pursuing wealth, comfort, status, variety and amusements on a grand scale. One gets the impression that in liberating Western Europe from a great part of the responsibility for self-defense, the US also unburdened Western Europeans of a sense of seriousness regarding the fate of their national communities. Generally speaking, national ideals were jettisoned in the 78-year period since the end of the War. World War II marked not only the defeat of Nazi Germany. Germany went down, but so too, did the rest of the nation-states of Europe. The continental-sized powers, shored up by their universal doctrines, triumphed over German nationalism.

Now the only way that the European nations can avoid cultural assimilation through Western or Eurasian globalization is to form a common front against globalization, both as a concrete expression of overwhelming geopolitical power and an ideal. Europeans should learn that the striving for world unification, whether of the Western or Eurasian variety, is not a pathway to universal sweetness and light, but rather a process leading to excessive and dangerous concentration of power on a worldwide scale. We are not talking about the current European Union, which is merely an instrument of Western globalization. The EU elites are clearly intent on totally assimilating the European peoples through the promotion of a massive influx of tens of millions, if not eventually hundreds of millions, of poverty-stricken African and Asian migrants.

Our globalist counterparts have seized the reins of power and now control enormous masses of people and the material resources of entire continents. Their mighty propaganda apparatus constantly reminds Europeans about the vast destruction of both world wars and the alleged role that European nation-state patriotism played in unleashing these disasters. This demoralizes European patriots and makes them more receptive to the appeals of universal doctrines like Marxism and neo-liberalism. Too many well-intentioned Europeans are ready to condemn what they are told is "national egoism." The frequent references to the tragic outcomes of the wars also make the subtle point that European nation-states are too weak to oppose the will of the empire builders.

If the European nation-states were to regain their sovereignty in the future, they should at all costs avoid any thought of territorial revisions. The renewal of territorial claims would greatly harm the interests of a Europe of national states situated in a world of giant superpowers. Continental-sized countries outside of Europe would certainly exploit tensions arising from territorial disputes to block effective collective security arrangements. Any political force advocating territorial revision in Europe would be pursuing short-term advantages that would be disastrous for all Europeans in the long term.

The Gdansk/Danzig issue of 1939 ought to serve as a clear warning about the potential of even small territorial disputes to draw into European affairs much stronger powers which are not necessarily interested in perpetuating European nation-states. In the 21st century Europe is not strong enough to ignore this danger. European nation-states were already standing on the abyss in 1939, and the danger signals were apparent already in 1918.

I believe that the aforementioned considerations about the decline of European nation-states, as well as the geopolitically extremely alarming developments that bear strong similarities to recent history, must have motivated Stefan Korte to write this highly relevant book within the context of the Ukrainian war. I have known and worked with the author for six years, and can attest that Stefan Korte is as sincere and dedicated a fighter for German and European values as one can hope to find in an age marked by cynicism and political opportunism.

There are so many issues involved in the current Ukrainian crisis. But for European patriots the main challenge should be to conceive of and forge foreign and defence policies which will ultimately serve the national interests of the separate European nations, and not the long-term goals of the empire builders, whether they be of the Western or Eastern stamp. In my opinion, the United States and NATO currently still have the task of maintaining the balance of power on the European continent. Given the ever closer cooperation between Russia and China, would it not be more reasonable to consider the US and NATO as the lesser of two challenges to Europeans' freedom of action?

Algis Avizienis
US-Diplomat (ret.) Eastern Europe
Head of the Lithuanian Investment Agency (ret.)

Preface by the author

First, I would like to thank you for taking the time to read this book. It has been written with the aim of familiarising the reader with some of the main geopolitical developments and projects that currently and directly affect us in Europe, and to explain what geopolitics is all about. The aim is to focus on events and, above all, the background to them, which are reported on, little or not at all in the leading European media, which primarily give the impression of being an enforced conform media, and when they are reported on these subjects, it is usually in a one-sided manner. This one-sidedness gives the impression that the media products are sometimes manipulative or indoctrinating content that is obviously not intended to actually and comprehensively inform us. This is to prevent the responsible citizen and voter from being able to form his or her own opinion based on knowledge or insight.

For decades we have been increasingly deprived of the possibility of critically evaluating information. This faculty assumes the ability to take in information from a variety of sources, which may well include one's own experience. It presupposes an objective assessment of facts and events. It is increasingly important for the citizen to maintain a healthy dose of scepticism. He must be able to read between the lines and independently supplement what has been concealed through his own research. The politically conscious citizen must be vigilant to avoid being duped by the state and corporate media, which aim at replacing cognition and knowledge with assumption and belief. Media competence is often invoked, but it does not seem to be really desired. This may sound to some like the often admonishing "conspiracy theory" or hysteria of "extremists", but that is precisely not what it is: as a mature and critical citizen, it is significant not to completely push aside mentally what is considered impossible, but to consider it attentively as an equal possibility. In order to achieve all this, it is first necessary to find the courage to maintain oppositional thinking or to acquire it again. This applies to all issues and policy fields, and not only to foreign policy. In most European countries, we are currently facing a progressive division of societies, which is particularly true for Germany. The maxim of "divide and rule" seems to be systematically applied, because a disunited people are a weak people. Weak and disunited peoples are correspondingly easier to manipulate and do not offer any serious resistance because they are no longer capable of doing so, due to their mental condition.

We can easily understand the division and hostility in Germany, for example, in a growing number of fault lines: the policy on foreigners, asylum and immigration, the relationship with Russia and the Russia sanctions, the so-called climate policy – "man-made climate change" and the declared danger from carbon dioxide, the meaning, and consequences of the energy turnaround, the "COVID-19 protection measures" in all their manifestations up to the deprivation of fundamental rights laid down in the constitution and the compulsion to vaccinate with insufficiently tested preparations. These are just a few examples of how society in Germany is being divided. This process is a European problem that we find in every country of our cherished continent. A problem that we may only be able to solve together. In addition to those mentioned, we are now faced with another line of division. Once again, it is massively fuelled by the leading media and the majority of politicians from parliaments and governments; we are talking about the relationship with the USA, NATO, and Russia. What role do these powers play – who is the villain, and who is up to good and right? Opinions differ and people bang their heads verbally about whether the USA/NATO or Russia is or should be our ally. The question, in all its complexity and opaque backgrounds, is at best insufficiently answerable. One should therefore be wary of jumping to conclusions or purely trusting something that is presented to us through the media and politicians' speeches. It is surely the worst way to give pure faith to these persons, when what should matter is the recognition of truth and reality. In order to focus on the current and essential events, many important points had to be presented in a condensed form and further details had to be omitted. It was essential to go into the things that are currently critical for Europe and for our future, because they are likely to have far-reaching effects. Geopolitics and the geostrategic goals are of some influence on our lives to an extent that many of us are not aware of. How much geopolitics determines everyone's circumstances and future, what geopolitics is, how to recognise geopolitical aspirations and actions, and what we can expect from certain developments will be addressed here.

The subject is anything but easy to survey, let alone to see through. For this reason this book is written from an empirical, very pragmatic point of view. I have used my experiences from my work in the German Bundestag, the many political trips to Eastern Europe and the invaluable and interesting conversations I have had with numerous people from politics, media and business as the basis for this book; the impetus for the work thus came from my own experiences and from the realisation that it is precisely this information that should be made available to a wider public. The book will provide a theoretical understanding of geopolitics in a short chapter, but is essentially intended to present this instrument in its practical implementation and effects. It will try to explain connections, which in turn should make it possible to draw conclusions from the identified geopolitical symptom to the possible causes and connections, or the originator(s).

Although the focus will be on Eastern Europe, the methodology of geopolitics is the same everywhere; it repeats itself. Once one has developed a basic understanding of how geopolitics works, which powers make use of it, then one recognises it everywhere in the world and also the handwriting of those who devised it.

The subject is exceedingly complex when presented and viewed as a whole. Much more complicated than it would be possible to present it fully comprehensively on 230 pages; for this reason, of course, no claim can be made to completeness. On the contrary, the modest approach is to provide the reader with hints and food for thought so that they will be able to recognise negative political developments more quickly. Understanding current and upcoming political developments can most definitely have a positive impact on one's own life and environment. By understanding an impending situation early on, one's actions can shift from pure reaction to action. Being able to make decisions before being caught cold by geopolitical events is the small but crucial advantage in the challenging wild times ahead.

In the future, this book and also the planned supplements and extensions on specific topics will concentrate on the geographical area of "Eastern Europe" and deviate from it in exceptional cases.

So if there is anything missing from this edition, it may follow in one of the future multipage supplements or on the website. Should you yourself be interested in a special topic or wish to share important information, knowledge or valid sources on the matters mentioned here, I would also be pleased to receive suggestions from you. This book is due for a complete revision in about a year's time. The next edition will then contain much more historical background, background information and further subject areas and new sources. At this stage, however, as already mentioned, topicality was much more significant to me than scope.

Sincerely yours

Stefan Korte
Lauchhammer, Germany,
30th of May 2023.

Introduction

Our times have become short-lived, world events unmanageable, opaque and even the decisions in politics at the national level leave the ordinary citizen with more questions than could have been answered by press release or government declaration. Institutions like the European Union, which will be discussed later, are theoretically problem enough for a Europe of self-determined nations. Never-ending centralisation processes, sweeping regulations down to the local level, the transformation of Europe into a supranational state, a misguided refugee policy and an inflationary financial system dominated the political picture until the end of 2019. At the beginning of 2020, Covid-19 was added and with it an unprecedented restrictive lockdown policy, which in retrospect turned out to be disproportionate and disastrous for the economy of all European countries. In this context, one realises how little these measures and the behaviour of politicians at all levels had to do with democracy. They used the fear of the people to make them compliant.

At the time, it was thought that these measures could no longer be surpassed in terms of negligence, but then came the Ukraine war. With it came the realisation that there is always more to everything, especially when politicians are involved in important decisions who have lost all contact with the people on the street due to chronic blindness and deafness. Parties and politicians then showed their true colours. The Greens in Germany showed their colours already shortly after the election and mutated into the eco-fascists that many in the country had thought they were, for some time. Now, in addition, they have become the number one warmonger in Germany and the fight to the last bullet against Russia has become the overshadowing agenda of the green global socialists. The opinion of their own people has long since ceased to interest the Green leaders. But first, before we dig deep into the geopolitics of Europe, let's have a brief look at the current politics in Germany. A policy that is supported to far too great an extent by the once conservative CDU (Christian Democratic Union), is in the process of ruining Germany socially and economically. What Merkel started slowly in the previous 16 years is now being completed at an exponentially increased speed. What this policy is doing to the people of Germany is becoming increasingly clear, at least for all those with life experience and a minimum of basic education and who pay some attention to their surroundings... Increased energy costs are leading to rising unemployment, as gas and electricity in particular have now become the biggest cost factor for many companies. Private households are also strongly affected by the immense price increases.

The social and economic upheavals are now clearly evident everywhere. The downward spiral in the country is thus turning faster and faster. Where is the urgently needed countermeasure by the federal government with a sense of proportion? All hot air and nothing happened, at least nothing in the sense of the own population. Nothing that alleviates the worries and needs of the people in Germany. The government continues to let thousands of refugees from Africa and the Middle East into the country. Not a day goes by that these people are not conspicuous by violence against Germans and also against their own countrymen. Murder, manslaughter, and rape have become the order of the day in Germany. Hundreds of millions of euros of taxpayers' money are spent on integration and qualifications, most of which do not have the desired effect. The German taxpayer is liable for all these monstrosities. Aid programmes for citizens, based on an energy and economic policy that can only be described as insane, can at best be described as half-hearted. These programs are far too long in coming and fizzle out without having brought about even a hint of improvement for the people in the country. An example of this would be the "relief package". For the readers outside Germany, this package was put together by the federal government to ease the burden on citizens. It included a reduction in the price of petrol and diesel by €0.30 and €0.14 respectively for a three-month period. A one-off payment of €300 for employees, which had to be taxed. A one-time child bonus of €100 and a €9 monthly rail ticket for 3 months.

A large part of the current problems are based on the morbid idea that Russia can be defied in the energy sector. Germany, which itself has hardly any natural resources and whose economy is dependent on cheap energy in order to remain competitive on the globalised market, despite its technological lead, is acting like a world power. It has to be said in all clarity that the federal government is throwing good and solid economic relations and a long-term secure energy supply out the window without having any alternative. At least none that is affordable for the citizens and will not cost thousands of jobs. In comparison, this is as tired of life as jumping out of an aeroplane knowing that you don't have a parachute with you but thinking that you will surely find a solution on your way down.

The situation is similar in the European Union. While things were coming to a head in Eastern Europe, the EU itself preferred to deal with gender studies, LGBTQ rights, an irresponsible financial policy and supported the illegal smuggling of refugees across the Mediterranean to Italy and defined the future of Europe at their own discretion in a conference that was supposed to present the opinion of the people of Europe transparently and democratically, but was in fact light years away from it. Instead of mediating between the warring parties, Ukraine was promised rapid membership in the EU, which was later relativised. In the meantime, the European Union has degenerated into an entity that, like NATO after the fall of the Iron Curtain, is looking for a reason to exist. The people in Eastern Europe have completely different ideas about how their society should develop, especially with regard to their own culture and values. Its the same in the west, there are more and more voices openly asking why the EU has to influence everything and everyone, and they are beginning to categorically reject this kind of totalitarianism. Over the decades, the once so sensible European economic community has become a gathering place for discarded politicians, corrupt functionaries, narcissists, and incompetents.

COVID-19 and the whole political caste have harmed the entire continent with their confused and largely anti-democratic decisions. With the war now raging in Ukraine and the economic and financial challenges it poses, Europe is in the midst of its biggest crisis since World War II. None of those responsible has the necessary foresight and wisdom to react adequately to this situation. Instead, the cart is being pulled deeper and deeper into the mud, and the dangers for the continent are growing by the day. Europe is currently changing faster than at any time since the end of the Second World War. The processes that have been set in motion are not accidental, they are based on geostrategic planning, which is the foundation of successful geopolitics.

What is geopolitics?

Geopolitics stands for geographical politics, which is a component of foreign politics and refers in its analysis to geographic, economic and military conditions. However, it is not actually a policy in the familiar sense. Indeed, the general term politics is misleading here, because geopolitics is in fact a science, originally derived from political geography. It was considered, especially at the beginning of the 20th century, as an analytical tool for political processes that had to do primarily with geographical conditions of a country or region. Geopolitics represents, so to speak, the link between geography and foreign politics strategy. It is based on the fact that all international politics, from peace to war, are divided into and takes place in time and space, in clearly defined geographical areas and spaces.

Geopolitical actors are concerned with the political influence and domination of geographical areas, and thus seek to create a spatial order according to their ideas. The definition of space in geopolitics does not refer to the entire earth's space, but to political subspaces and thus also to their borders and their shifts in the past and future. In these geographical spaces, which represent territories, countries and continents, individual spheres of interest or also called spheres of influence are formed from the different interests of states, whether political, economic or other. Geopolitics is the tool to assert these interests.

Geopolitics is the appropriate tool for analysing circumstances and subsequently effectively implementing one's own predefined interests. The way there is often a long-term process, usually over decades, which requires a series of actions at the most diverse political and social levels. As a rule, no consideration is given to the sensitivities, interests, or needs of others.

As mentioned above, a certain power is needed to be able to conduct geopolitics, which is why it is usually the great powers that can exert influence on other states. However, depending on the geographical, cultural, political or economic circumstances, less influential states can also assert spheres of interest. In the end, however, the question remains to what extent they can actually assert themselves against the interests of the major powers. Spheres of influence of different states can relate to the same areas. The resulting overlaps in spheres of interest can be used to common advantage or lead to conflicts of interest, which in turn can be resolved either through diplomacy or military force.

There are great powers that claim exclusive spheres of interest for themselves, in which they do not tolerate any interference by other states. If this is not respected, it can even mean war in the worst case scenario. A very good example of this is the United States of America. James Monroe, US president from 1817 to 1825, produced a doctrine, that defined the continent of North and South America as an exclusively US sphere of interest. The Monroe Doctrine is still valid today and is also stringently pursued by the USA. In the course of this book, we will come back to this doctrine more often.

Space in geopolitical thinking has two aspects. A geometric and a geographical one. The geometric aspect is primarily concerned with the shape, structure, and location of space and with parts of space. To put it more figuratively, it is about the consideration of states and parts of states. The geographical aspect is much more important in our consideration. This is where the natural and cultural character-istics of space come into play. Rivers, lakes, mountains and vegetation, as well as people, economy, infrastructure and ruling order. The geopolitical dimension of space is followed by the dimension of time due to a physical inevitability. Time is a factor that has steadily gained importance in geopolitics over the past decades as technology has increased. It is therefore hardly surprising that the speed

Friedrich Ratzel

with which a multitude of information is exchanged and disseminated today is an important factor in geostrategic considerations. However, modern geopolitics must take other essential factors into account if it is to be truly effective. These include globally active institutions and "think tanks", environmental influences and climate-related changes, economic issues arising from the globalised world and globally active individuals with considerable influence. In Germany, the term geopolitics was avoided for decades for historical reasons. It was felt that the instrumentalisation by the National Socialists had discredited the term and the empirical considerations behind it. In Germany, with its wide-spread do-gooderism and tendency to self-mutilate its own achievements, values and history, no-one seems to realise that this is nonsense. Geopolitics was practiced by all great powers such as the USSR, Great Britain, China, and the

Rudolf Kjellen

23

USA, but none of these powers had the idea of discrediting an entire branch of science, because of the crimes of Stalin, Churchill, Mao or Roosevelt. The term geopolitics and the science behind it simply remain exactly what it is, a science and not a religion or world view. Although the National Socialists may have been the first to implement their policies through geostrategic considerations in a targeted and partially successful manner, but they didn't invent or develop it further in essential features.

The foundation for geopolitics as we know it was laid before World War I by the German zoologist and geographer Friedrich Ratzel in 1897, who was responsible for reforming political geography. The term geopolitics itself, however, was coined by the Swede Rudolf Kjellén in 1899. Kjellen was in turn inspired by Ratzel in his reflections. In 1916, he wrote: "Geopolitics is the study of the state as a geographical organism or as a phenomenon in an area".[1]

The German Karl Haushofer (1869 – 1946) ultimately based his reflections on the theories of Ratzel, Kjellen and Mackinder (more on him later). His theory of the "Lebensraum" for the geographical organism (the state) power-political considerations, in relations between great powers and smaller states, was an essential building block of National Socialist geopolitics. The latest scientific research and findings have shown, however, that Haushofer's involvement with the National Socialists and his reputation as the intellectual ori-

Karl Haushofer

[1] Der Staat als Lebensform. Hirzel, Leipzig 1917

ginator of imperial-aggressive aspirations was greatly overrated and exploited for populist purposes, especially in Germany in the 1950s and 1960s. The geopolitical considerations were less interesting to Hitler than his personal thoughts on ideas of race. Haushofer was a recognised expert on Japan, a brilliant geologist and instrumental in establishing good relations with Japan. He produced some important works on geopolitics in the Pacific region in his time.

The following is an own definition of geopolitics:

Geopolitics is a space related, power-oriented foreign policy. If necessary, it can be enforced against emerging resistance, in order to create or improve the political and economic influence of a state on a specific geographical area or region.

Who practices geopolitics in Europe?

In principle, geopolitics can be practiced by any state on earth. However, in order to be successful in its implementation, some essential things are needed. These include, in particular, resources, strong military, economic and technological capabilities and a not insignificant diplomatic influence. The three big geopolitical players are, you will guess, the USA, China, and Russia.

The great, once influential states of Europe play only a minor role in the current geopolitical world. Neither the United Kingdom nor France leave a lasting mark on Europe, let alone the world, through their foreign policy. What about the largest economic power on the European continent? Germany, the country at the heart of Europe, which continues to lead in many areas of research, science, and industry? German foreign policy, if one can call it that at all, shines with a pronounced facelessness, and this is not only recently, but for several decades. German foreign ministers have become nodders of a USA geopolitics that can now only be described as dangerous and is not limited to the European continent. They are also trying to expand their spheres of influence in Asia and thus to block China from pursuing its own geopolitical aspirations. This is a major reason why tensions between the USA and China have been noticeably increasing for some time now.

The European Union, as a quasi-federal entity with great power airs, does not make a better impression than the individual states already mentioned. It is light years away from having its own geo-strategy as well as a foreign policy guided by common interests. But let's hear from someone who knows what he is talking about. Former American presidential advisor and alliance expert Zbigniew Brzeziński, who said the following in an interview about the EU when asked about the voice of Europe:

"I hear only timid voices and cacophony. There is no unity among European leaders. Are the Europeans really ready to stand up seriously to Tehran or even to stand up to America for a change? Do they have a strategic consensus? We Americans have learned that we cannot shape the world without Europe - but we have also learned that there is no one Europe that we can take seriously. So we have no partners."

This statement is self-explanatory in itself. America sees itself as superior to Europe because of Europe's political incompetence and the collective inconsistency that goes with it. It does not see the EU or individual states as partners in a united Europe. America believes it can shape the world according to its own ideas, but it knows that this cannot be done without

Europe. However, depending on the goal to be achieved, the necessary temporary helpers are chosen. The EU as an institution is tolerated by the USA because its own inconsistency makes it easy to control. The given ideals of the American idea of freedom and democracy are at least outwardly represented by the EU, even though its own structure acts increasingly undemocratically and intransparently and no longer lives up to the principles of the rule of law. Since we know who holds the geopolitical reins in Europe, it is not difficult to assess where in Europe there is currently the most geopolitical activity. However, there are also some side issues that are hardly mentioned in the media at the moment, but which can quickly mutate into a full-blown conflict. On the one hand, there is the extremely tense relationship between Turkey and Greece. The Turkish president's threatening gestures[2] have been hard to miss lately, but NATO does not seem to be interested at the moment in whether two member states might get into an armed conflict. The question of which ally would then receive support from which ally remains exciting, or whether the

Zbigniew Brzeziński 1928 -2017, (see Photo Credits page)

[2] https://www.politico.eu/article/erdogan-warns-greece-that-turkish-missiles-can-reach-athens%EF%BF%BC/

other NATO members will first wait until the UN Security Council tries to bring about a peaceful solution, which easily could take months.

It is noticeable to the observer that Turkey and especially Recep Tayyip Erdoğan come across as very arrogant. Turkey is currently refusing to agree to Sweden's accession to NATO for purely religious reasons. In this way, one puts one's own religious sensitivities, which have long since had no place in Western politics, against the security interests of an entire nation and tries to force concessions out of the Swedes, which apparently succeeds.[3]

In this context, it is appropriate to mention the Turkish intervention in Syria, where the Turkish army is attacking Kurdish positions. Turkey accuses the Kurds, without providing any evidence, of being responsible for attacks in Turkey and invokes the right of peoples to self-defence under the UN Charter for the "retaliatory actions" carried out. The problem is that this right to self-defence is conditional. This means that certain conditions must be met in order to invoke it. In principle, the authors of the Charter assumed that an "armed attack" must be carried out by one state against another. Since the terrorist attack of 11th September 2001, however, acts of violence by non-state actors such as terrorist organisations also be considered "armed attacks". Here, however, the legal situation is much more complicated, as the extent of the attack plays a significant role in the assessment and, in the context of self-defence, the territory of another state is violated which may have nothing to do with the attacks. Syria, in that regard, has nothing to do with the alleged Kurdish attacks on Turkish territory. The burden of proof here lies with the one who invokes the right to

---

[3] https://apnews.com/article/nato-politics-turkey-government-recep-tayyip-erdogan-f9a568da05914a4143a033e74067b6f4

self-defence. Turkey has so far failed to provide this evidence in its actions, which are disproportionate to the terrorist acts committed. That such behaviour is incompatible with the principles of our enlightened and secularised Western world needs no further explanation. That NATO and the USA tolerate such behaviour is incomprehensible and shows that, in the absence of possibilities, one is willing to fall back on a certain double standard a la the USA. One thing is certain, however: if you have such allies, you really don't need any more enemies.

Another hotspot that is hardly noticed at the moment is the Balkans. The Chinese are currently very busy massively expanding their influence there. The Chinese are taking a slightly different approach than the US. There is less emphasis on diplomacy and more on economic development and cooperation. EU-funded bridge projects are being implemented by Chinese companies. The Chinese are trying to keep capital flowing out of Europe. The US will start to flex its geopolitical muscles there in the not too distant future, not so much because of lost profits, but rather because of China's growing influence. Another reason could be that the Qataris have discovered Bosnia as a new field of activity for themselves. However, this could become more of a problem for Europe than for the USA. It seems that Islamic terrorism is being financed from there. Furthermore, a not inconsiderable number of companies are founded there by Qataris. This enables them to acquire real estate in Bosnia, which is something that foreigners are not allowed have. Another advantage is that foreign entrepreneurs can acquire Bosnian citizenship after 6-8 years of activity in Bosnia. This automatically increases one's influence on the country through the possibility of being elected to political office and even the path to the EU Parliament is wide open.

Recognising US geopolitics

We remember that in geopolitics, everything starts with a good geostrategy for a certain geographical space and with a clearly defined goal. Geopolitics is power politics aimed at either opening up new spheres of interest or expanding existing ones. With this in mind, it is relatively easy to see that geopolitics is an essential part of the USA foreign policy, which is understandable from an American perspective. The USA sees itself as the sole hegemon. The last remaining superpower on the planet. The geopolitical interests of China and Russia are perceived by the USA as revisionist. It sees itself challenged by them and threatened in its own claim to leadership. The idea that Russia and China could change the international order in their favour runs fundamentally counter to the traditional geopolitical interests of the USA. A cornerstone of USA geopolitics is to prevent states such as Russia and/or China from expanding their spheres of influence into an area to which the USA has already laid some kind of quasi-claim.

What the USA obviously sometimes does not really want to see is the fact, that these two massive states also have geostrategic interests and needs, which are undoubtedly different from those of the USA. Though they have nevertheless an equal right to exist and develop their spheres of interest, in view of the nuclear weapons, their economic power, the wealth of resources and their diplomatic influence of these great powers. The sometimes seemingly ignorant behaviour of the USA, with its doctrine of peace through strength, harbours a very high potential for conflict, as Russia and China may well perceive this behaviour as a threat.

The former assumption that the USA would accept so-called de facto spheres of influence, buffer zones - in the sense of global co-operation and in order to avoid the risk of war with Russia and China is now obsolete. On the basis of geography, state borders and evolved cultural spheres of influence, this would not only have been urgently necessary, it would also have been a logical and rational solution to minimise tensions between the superpowers. Thus, at the latest since the intensive efforts of Eastern European states to move into NATO's sphere of influence, which they were also encouraged to do from the onset, tensions have certainly increased. This especially applies to Taiwan and the massive military presence of the USA in the Western Pacific.

The obvious refusal on the part of the USA to reach what we might call a geopolitical understanding, as well as the introduction of prioritised spheres of influence, notwithstanding their own, leads to a greatly increased potential for conflict. Especially in view of the very different ideas and needs and in view of the great military potential of all three protagonists. In this context, it does not remain hidden to the observer that many activities of the USA are currently designed to create further bilateral tensions. The idea of de-escalation does not seem to be on the USA's geopolitical agenda.

Already during Donald Trump's presidency, the US national security strategy was geared towards viewing China and Russia as a challenge and growing power rivalry. In their view, the integration of the two states into international institutions had not been successful. Sooner or later, the two powers would try to take back the geopolitical advantages the USA had achieved and thus attempt to change the international order in their favour.

Europe in the geopolitical headlock of the USA?

We have realised that the USA is not willing to accept another great power with conflicting interests, even if the geographical area in question is in another hemisphere. This means that strategies must be devised to consistently and effectively prevent the emergence of a rival from the outset. It should be noted that the USA would most probably not even accept another superpower with the same interests, as it would also be seen as a competitor and potential danger, as its geopolitical orientation could change at any time. That this is the case can be illustrated relatively well by the example of the European Union. The EU seems to be a close ally of the USA. They always agree when it comes to democracy and human rights, and economic cooperation is unblemished. At least as long as secret CIA prisons in Europe or human rights violations in Guantánamo are not mentioned and import duties to Europe are kept low. Meanwhile, the EU sees itself as a budding great power and wants to abolish the European nation states in the foreseeable future, in the interest of a multinational federal state of Europe. With this great power fantasy, it is now dreaming of its own geopolitical goals, which are currently still limited to the expansion of one's own spheres of influence through constant expansion. The USA is well aware of this potential danger and considers it an unacceptable risk. For this reason, it is important for the USA to maintain its existing influence over Europe. The simple strategy is to keep Europe occupied with itself. This is achieved mainly through individual agreements with European states, which in turn create disharmony within the European Union. Supporting alternative projects that could have a continental influence as well as destabilising the entire continent are also methods that the

USA has already used elsewhere in the past. Europe must under no circumstances become independent, especially at the present time, nor shall it develop its own ideas for a European foreign policy with its own interests, which could even be directed against the interests of the USA. The next important point in the strategy is to keep NATO alive and to guarantee the structure a long-term raison d'être.

Here, too, I would like to let Zbigniew Brzeziński, who has already been quoted once, have his say:

"NATO provides not only the institutional framework for the exercise of American influence in European affairs but also the basis for the politically decisive military presence of the USA in Western Europe. In the course of European unification, however, this defence structure will have to be adapted to the new reality of the Alliance, which is based on a more or less equal partnership and is no longer an alliance in which there is, to use traditional terms, a hegemon and a vassal ... A real choice for a united Europe will consequently force a far-reaching reorganisation of NATO, which will inevitably weaken the supremacy of the US within the Alliance."

For this reason alone, a frequently discussed reorganisation of NATO is something that the USA will never allow, especially in regard to the threat of losing its hegemonic position. In order to keep NATO alive, an enemy image is needed. This fell away with the collapse of the Soviet Union. China was not an option, as it was too far outside the originally envisaged field of activity. At that time, there was no threat in Europe that would have justified maintaining NATO indefinitely. While tensions in the former Yugoslavia increased in the years between 1991 and 1999, a new strategy was being refined at NATO headquarters. In future, it should be possible for NATO to engage militarily outside its own territory. These missions were defined as "out of area". The result of this first mission of this kind is certainly still fresh in many people's memories. The bombing of Yugoslavia (Serbia) without a valid UN mandate is still highly disputed under international law. And for all those who may have forgotten, I would like to recall how the German Greens Party mutated into warmongers of the finest order back then, when they were first allowed to taste the sweet taste of government power. It was Joschka Fischer, former minister of foreign affairs, who, in sports palace style, got the German Bundestag on track with pithy slogans. Never again National Socialism, never again Auschwitz, are only two examples of his agitation skills.[4]

Europe is currently standing there geopolitically with its trousers down. Unable to speak with one voice, it has no European foreign policy concept of its own. Let alone a geopolitical strategy. In terms of defence policy, it is on the wrong track for quite some time now (EU army) and so it dutifully follows the hegemon's lead and does what it is told. Perhaps we, as Europeans, should firstly state that the sovereignty of European nations is not a matter of negotiation, not for anyone. And it is not being played geopolitical roulette with, certainly not by an "ally" who obviously does not have our best interests in mind. That would be a start, and possibly a healthy basis for a foreign policy of our own. One guided by European interests.

---

[4] https://www.spiegel.de/politik/ich-darf-nicht-wackeln-a-a378fb47-0002-0001-0000-000010932908

German foreign policy at rock bottom

To the outside observer, it appears that German foreign policy makers have been given little opportunity to pursue their own country's interests in a sovereign manner since the end of the Second World War. This impression may not be entirely dismissed, for the only geopolitical thing Germany did after the end of the Second World War, was to strive for the re-establishment of German unity. Even that was torpedoed several times by the occupying powers and in the final instance only implemented under their strict conditions.. Due to the occupation statutes, essential and landmark decisions always required the consent of the Allied forces. It was soon made clear by the WWII Allies that re-unification with the GDR had to exclude recovery of the German provinces in the east. One might have assumed that, at least after reunification, the foreign policy of a sovereign country would take a more offensive stance and represent its own interests more consistently, but this was not the case. One always followed the geopolitical compass of the USA and did what the EU decided in its socialist-like committees. And the EU in turn followed the instructions of the United States without any objections. The evidence for this follows in the following chapters.

The foreign policy of the Federal Republic of Germany became more and more meaningless from election period to election period. With the SPD's Heiko Maas[5], it already took on a tragicomic character and now, with the Green's Annalena Bearbock, it ended in a grotesque spectacle where the comic met the ghastly. Sovereignty is missing here, as is a backbone and expertise. That Germany does not have a foreign policy guided by its own interests is bad enough, but with the current occupation within

---

[5] German Minister of Foreign Affairs 2018 - 2021

the German Foreign Ministry, things are becoming worrying. To put it bluntly, Germany is making a fool of itself on the international stage. At the same time, the behaviour of the Green Foreign Minister, in her diplomatic doltishness, is dangerous when, for example, she declares, seemingly without any preconceived ideas, that we are in a war against Russia. Which, on the one hand, is wrong and, on the other, could be interpreted by the Russian side as an unofficial declaration of war. Such a statement by a supposedly well-versed expert in international law is quite remarkable. It is equally remarkable that such a statement, in this day and age, at least in the Western world, does not cause much of a stir and does not entail any consequences for the minister in question. It is easy for rational people to understand that Russia is using this statement by the highest German diplomat for its own propaganda and is not particularly pleased with such rhetoric. One hundred years ago, this statement would have caused a full-blown diplomatic crisis and, without a well-considered apology, would probably have led to worse. Foreign policy stands or falls on skilful diplomacy, which depends to a large extent on well-thought-out, implied rhetoric. Today, however, this understanding no longer seems to exist. Even before the outbreak of the war in Ukraine, in February 2022, it was diplomatically unskilful to visit Warsaw and Kiev before Moscow. Such behaviour suggests that Ms Baerbock has her own idea of diplomacy, or may have allowed herself to be pressured into such an act. In any case, the diplomatic belittling of Moscow was the result of this behaviour.

Annalena Baerbock stated in an interview in 2021 that the most important task of diplomacy is to prevent and contain crises and to solve them in the best possible way. This sounds nice at first, but it ignores the essential point: the central task of diplomacy is to protect the interests of one's own country, to represent them and to negotiate accordingly. In communication, diplomacy means using a form of expression that does not unnecessarily attack or irritate the negotiating partner. That in her opinion the climate crisis is the most threatening of all crises is evidence of her ideological delusion and incompetence in matters of foreign policy.

In her latest stroke of genius, Ms Baerbock has now drastically lowered the requirements for diplomatic personnel.[6] An intensive test of general education and a psychological examination have been cancelled without replacement. The Foreign Minister has already made her idea of a feminist foreign policy public.[7] She wants to see more women in the diplomatic service. It is no coincidence that it was mostly women who failed the psychological evaluation. The fact that this has now been cancelled has, of course, nothing to do with this. At least, the way has been cleared for the post of "Foreign Office ambassador for feminist foreign policy".[8] The German Foreign Ministry is currently being transformed into a comedy aristocracy which, once completed, will provide unsurpassed amusement on the international stage, but can no longer be taken seriously by anyone. Thus, in its decline, the Foreign Ministry is following, with some delay, the example of the Defence Ministry, which has already undergone a corresponding transformation since the arrival of Ursula von der Leyen, Federal Minister of Defence from 2013 to 2019. India already made its disdain for Green Foreign Minister Baerbock clear when she arrived at the New Delhi airport for the G20 foreign ministers' meeting on 1st - 2nd March 2023 and no welcoming committee was ready or other diplomatic protocol fol-

---

[6] https://www.merkur.de/politik/csu-cdu-annalena-baerbock-diplomaten-test-regeln-neu-voraussetzung-deutschland-aenderung-kritik-91675636.html

[7] https://www.reuters.com/world/europe/germany-unveils-guidelines-give-foreign-policy-a-more-female-face-2023-03-01/

[8] https://www.news.de/politik/856768712/annalena-baerbock-leitlinien-katalog-fuer-feministische-aussenpolitik-kritik-an-vorschlag-der-gruenen-politikerin-auf-twitter-zerrissen/1/

lowed. The German Ambassador saved Ms Baerbock from getting lost on the airport premises. The extent to which people's perceptions diverge in such an incident is quite remarkable. There are actually people who write the following on Twitter:[9]

"She is doing well, even if she is greeted and picked up too late. She is handling the situation well. Very friendly, confident and above the faux pas. Perfect"

"Baerbock has real Star Wars senator vibes and that's freaking cool"

"Well, I guess that's the new feminist protocol. Walks out of the machine completely unassuming on her own and apparently surprises the whole welcoming delegation that she's been there a long time. She's quite impressive."

How far away from reality do you have to be to write comments like that? If one now compares the arrival of the Russian Foreign Minister, Sergei Lavrov, in India on the same occasion with Baerbock's, it is obvious that far more people, including the press, had an interest in attending it. In addition, Lavrov was received by a large diplomatic contingent as guest of honour. To make matters worse, the German Foreign Minister used the economic meeting to present her demands for an end to the war in Ukraine to Lavrov, without making any concrete proposals herself and without giving due consideration to Ukraine's rejection of peace talks. This is also the reason why Lavrov apologised afterwards to the host country, India, for Ms Baerbock's behaviour. One does not have to side with the Russians, but observance of diplomatic etiquette, which does not allow for

---

[9] https://www.news.de/politik/856775774/annalena-baerbock-amuesiert-sich-ueber-protkoll-fauxpas-in-neu-delhi-aussenministerin-ohne-begruessungskomitee-vorm-g20-gipfel/1/

non-subject issues to be raised at such meetings, should be both a duty and a freestyle at this level. Ms Baerbock failed all along the line here!

What if Germany had pursued its own foreign policy guided by geo-strategic interests? Well, then Eastern Europe in particular would have been an extremely important area for establishing its own spheres of interest. Resources needed by German companies are stored there. There are lucrative economic areas waiting to be developed, and there would be little to prevent the continuation of a tried and tested alliance policy to secure lasting peace on the European continent. It was this kind of German foreign policy that earned the Reich Chancellor Otto von Bismarck all the honours.

After the founding of the German Empire, in 1871, many of its European neighbours were concerned about the newly formed and greatly enlarged German Empire, now situated in the middle of Europe. This was due to its comparatively highly developed education and research system, almost inexhaustible coal reserves in Silesia, the Ruhr region, the Saarland, its burgeoning industry, as well as a state organisation that surpassed everything else. The main concern was the increased economic and military influence. This led to strong mistrust on the part of many European states. Above all, the major European powers of the time distrusted the united German Empire. Otto von Bismarck was acutely aware of this and, with the greatest diplomatic skill, tried to ease these tensions, always keeping the old enmities firmly in mind. He began to develop a complex system of alliances in order to preserve relations with other nations in a way that would serve the German Empire, but at the same time ensure security by balancing the forces. Bismarck wanted to prevent a two-front war at all costs. Germany would have been at the mercy of such a war if Great Bri-

Reichskanzler Otto Fürst von Bismarck in his study

tain or France had allied with Russia. He saw his most important task in preventing the emergence of such alliances. He was aware that there was only one logical approach to solving this problem, namely by including Russia in an alliance himself. It was clear to Bismarck that Russia, because of its size and wealth of resources, had to be fundamentally involved in European decision-making and development processes. A foreign policy of Germany or other Central European states against Russia would be to the disadvantage of all European states.

It is fair to say that Bismarck's German foreign policy was of the highest diplomatic quality, and that his name still has a good reputation today. The fact that the current Foreign Minister has the cheek to rename the traditional Bismarck Room in the Foreign Ministry shows not only a political narrow-mindedness, but also a historical disorientation. German foreign policy in Bismarck's time was characterised by an excellent knowledge of Eastern Europe. It knew the people, their characters, their peculiarities and strengths and, based on this, created a continental foreign policy that still enjoys the highest reputation in the world today. However, Germany has squandered much of this through short-sightedness. Especially after the Second World War and in a further push after reunification. There was too much fixation on Russia and China. The main buzzwords were cheap energy and outsourcing. People forgot what an important influence the Eastern European states have on the future of Germany and Europe. They preferred to sink their billions into structures like the EU, where the return for Germany is more than questionable. The beneficiary countries of the EU receive a tidy chunk of German tax money from Germany, the record net payer. However, we have never heard a thank you for this.

With regard to the war in Ukraine, from Germany's point of view there are two states in conflict, both of which are of economic importance to Germany: Russia as a reliable supplier of cheap energy sources and raw materials, and Ukraine, also a country with a wealth of resources and great potential for economic cooperation. Germany would have done well to take a neutral position in this conflict. From this position, it would have been a serious honest broker for both parties, able to mediate for the sake of peace while not considering Europe as its geopolitical playing field. Only from such a position, without sacrificing Germany's best economic relations with Russia, would there have been a solid basis for negotiations. Decades of work were sacrificed, without thinking. With its actions since February 2022, the German government has brilliantly placed itself between two stools and thus angered both sides. On the one hand, Russia, by breaking binding agreements that were an important part of a functioning economy for Germany and mostly had nothing to do with the arms industry. On the other hand, Ukraine, the USA and NATO by hesitating to cut certain ties and initially refusing to supply Ukraine with defence equipment.

With all that has been mentioned before, one must also speak of a historical duty of restraint on Germany's part in this conflict, which is otherwise demanded precisely by those who cannot get enough weapons and commitment now. In great contradiction to this were the almost hysterical and not very diplomatically presented demands of the former Ukrainian ambassador and actual vice foreign minister of Ukraine, Andrij Melnyk, who saw in Germany a historical duty and therefore demanded heavy weapons in the most penetrating way. One thing is certain: if, in view of past wars, Germany has a responsibility to exercise restraint and neutrality, then this applies to all sides, including Russia. However, it seems as if this has suddenly become obsolete with the invasion of Ukraine. German tanks in this region, directed against Russia, have a certain aftertaste, no matter how you spin it. Historical responsibility is absent from this German government. And of all people, those from the camp of the left-wing Red-Green chic, who never tire of pointing out in connection with domestic political disputes that one must learn from history, willingly brush aside this central idea. Even when it goes against their own German needs. It is equally surprising how flexible some Western states are in this context. Poland is a particularly striking example of an "ally" here, and never tires of reminding us of our historical responsibility and discrediting Germany wherever possible. Poland demands completely insane amounts of reparations from Germany, but when it comes to Russia, German intervention is virtually forced. Ultimately, all the former Western victorious powers can join this chorus of hypocrites. There is always a great clamour when Germany has an opinion of its own and has the cheek to defend it. If the Federal Republic does not do what is expected on the part of its allies, Germany quickly becomes an enemy again. We remember when former Chancellor Gerhard Schröder rejected German participation in the Iraq war in 2003 and the subsequent icy relationship of the USA towards Germany.[10] However, when Germany previously supported the bombing of Yugoslavia in violation of international law, also under the Red-Green government and the Green Foreign Minister Joschka Fischer, and participated with Tornados in combat operations without a UN mandate, everything was embedded in the finest harmony.[11] Mediation is only possible when both sides are open to arguments. This was already complicated at the beginning of the dispute between Russia and Ukraine, but at this point, in

[10] https://www.dw.com/en/schr%C3%B6der-rejects-war-that-will-kill-thousands-in-iraq/a-811719

[11] https://www.tagesspiegel.de/politik/nato-angriffe-zermurben-rot-grune-regierung-un-prangern-fluchtlingselend-an-597607.html

February 2023, a diplomatic solution seems to have receded into the distance.

Attack on Germany

An unimaginable act of terrorism against the Federal Republic of Germany occurred on 27th September 2022. On this day, both Nord Stream pipelines were blown up by unknown persons. It quickly became apparent from the damage that only an elaborate attack, with special military equipment and careful planning, could have destroyed three of the four Nord Stream pipes in this way, at a water depth of about 80 metres. It was now important to present the world with a culprit as quickly as possible. Surprisingly, the Norwegians, who are otherwise rarely involved in major world events, were very quick to find the culprit this time: It was, how could it be otherwise, the Russian himself. At least, that is the opinion of the Norwegian military scientist and naval officer, Ivar Strömmen. According to his account, only Russia had the means and a "plausible" reason to blow up the pipelines, which were financed and laid to a considerable extent by Russian funds.[12] His explanation for this: In this way, Russia wants to create sufficient legitimacy for itself that it is not currently supplying gas to Europe. One can only shake one's head at such a contrived and incomprehensible explanation. One can safely assume that no serious expert would voluntarily put forward such a rediculous conclusion without having a specific motivation. What drove Ivar Strömmen to do it? One can only speculate. Without further ado, let's look at the whole thing through the lens of criminology. In order to commit a crime of any kind, one needs a motive, the necessary means and an opportunity. Who else could be considered for this crime? From this point of view, at least one other suspect suggests itself: the USA. They would definitely have the motive for such a

[12] https://www.tagesschau.de/ausland/europa/nord-stream-eins-druckabfall-107.html

crime. For years, the Americans have been trying in vain to sell their own fracking gas at a high price. There are documents showing that the American government was willing to take the necessary measures in Europe to sell its energy resources. [13] The opportunity was certainly favourable at the time, even if it may seem a little too obvious. The fairy tale that the Russians destroyed their own pipeline is also contradicted by the dense maritime surveillance in the Baltic Sea, especially in the current situation.

The suspicion is corroborated by the words of Joe Biden, who actually formulated a solid confession to the press as early as January 2022.[14] He told the press that if the Russians invade Ukraine, there will be no more Nord Stream 2. When asked by a reporter how this would be done, since it was basically a project under German sovereignty, Biden replied that she could be sure that a way would be found. Victoria Nuland, US undersecretary of state for political affairs, made a similar announcement a few weeks earlier in a clearly understandable statement on the termination of Nord Stream.[15] So why has no one in the West officially thought of at least naming the USA as the culprit? However, one could also see a twist of fate in all this. Where one source dries up, under whatever circumstances, another one opens up as if by a "miracle". This was the case here. Just one day after this catastrophe, the new pipeline that was to carry gas from Norway to Poland opened.[16] Fate seems to have a good hand for "timing".

---

[13] https://www.reuters.com/business/energy/us-waive-sanctions-firm-ceo-behind-russias-nord-stream-2-pipeline-source-2021-05-19/

[14] https://www.youtube.com/watch?v=OS4O8rGRLf8

[15] https://www.youtube.com/watch?v=njJIJrAuniI

[16] https://www.reuters.com/markets/europe/gas-starts-flowing-poland-through-new-baltic-pipe-pipeline-2022-10-01/

At the time, it was not yet clear what would happen, but the events could not have coincided worse. On the same day, 26th September 2022, Russia once again clearly underlined the conditions for a nuclear first strike. The danger of an existential threat to Russia was clearly and unequivocally pointed out, for example through conventional weapons, which at that time and to this day are being delivered en masse to Ukraine, financed by European and American taxpayers. This act of sabotage can certainly be seen as an existential threat to Russia, as it makes it impossible to restart the pipelines indefinitely, even if the conditions for repairing them return to normal. The damage to Russia and to the Federal Republic of Germany, or to the Western companies involved, undoubtedly runs into the billions.

The Americans did not leave this threat unanswered for long. They announced that if the Russians used tactical nuclear weapons, the Americans, together with NATO, would destroy the Russians' entire Black Sea fleet and all conventional military equipment in the region. It was pointed out that this would not be a response under Article 5 of the NATO Treaty. It would be a separate response which, as in Yugoslavia and Libya before, would be an "out of area mission" and would most likely not be sanctioned by a UN mandate.[17] With regard to this attack against the Nord Stream pipelines, it must be said in all clarity that German interests were violated here. Germany suffered immense economic damage as a result. The fact that the act came from a state, or at least that it was commissioned by a state, is a point of view that causes little discussion even in the EU. The government spokesman of the German government, Steffen Hebestreit,

---

[17] https://www.theguardian.com/world/2022/oct/02/us-russia-putin-ukraine-war-david-petraeus

already made the following statement to RND (Redaktions Netzwerk Deutschland) on 27th September 2022:[18]

"This is speculation so far. Because of the great depth of the water, hobby divers or militant environmentalists are ruled out according to the assessment of security authorities. For such an attack, military capabilities are needed, they say. There is much to be said for a state actor".

The latest results of the Swedish investigation from the end of March 2023 also leave virtually no doubt that a state is behind these attacks on the Nord Stream pipelines.[19] This "rogue state" has without doubt carried out an act of war against the Federal Republic of Germany. But even the German government is too cowardly to state this fact openly. Instead, the rhetoric against Russia is becoming steadily harsher and the arms deliveries, at the expense of German taxpayers, are gaining momentum instead of coming to an end. What the established politicians apparently do not dare to explain must nevertheless be stated in no uncertain terms: The attack on the Nord Stream pipelines was an attack on Germany, aimed at hitting the economy hard and comprehensively. Even if Federal German government politicians claim otherwise and thus try to reassure the people of Germany, they are equally misleading. It is a fact that the failure of the Nord Stream pipelines makes calming down in the energy sector and the associated normalisation of energy costs impossible for the foreseeable future. The deliberate destabilisation of the German economy is apparently the desired consequence.

---

[18] https://www.zdf.de/nachrichten/politik/ylva-johansson-eu-sanktionen-ukraine-krieg-russland-100.html

[19] https://www.theguardian.com/world/2023/apr/06/nord-stream-sabotage-pipeline-blasts

To understand why the US is so highly suspicious of being involved in this attack in one way or another, one only has to look at the Americans' exasperation with the cheap, seemingly unlimited supply of Russian natural gas. Washington feared that as long as cheap natural gas was being delivered to Central Europe through the pipelines, countries like Germany might be reluctant to provide Ukraine with the money and weapons they felt they desperately needed to defeat Russia. This view is also held by investigative reporter Seymour Hersh, who caused a considerable stir at the end of February 2023 with a publication of alleged inside information.[20] Hersh reported that President Biden had instructed national security adviser Jake Sullivan to put together an inter-agency group to come up with a plan to eliminate this problem sustainably. All options should be on the table, but only one would come to fruition, Hersh said. Jake Sullivan was previously director of the US State Department's internal policy planning think tank under Barack Obama

Interestingly, there was already a very similar-looking project in 1971. At that time, the American intelligence services learned of a Russian submarine cable in the Sea of Okhotsk, which connected the naval headquarters in Vladivostok with a regional naval command and over which, surprisingly, unencrypted communication took place. The Russians were apparently a little too sure that no one would be able to intercept this. A team of specialists from the CIA and the NSA were tasked with developing a plan to tap this cable. Using naval divers, converted submarines and a deep-sea rescue craft, the Americans finally managed to locate the Russian cable. The divers attached a sophisticated listening device to the cable that

---

[20] https://seymourhersh.substack.com/p/how-america-took-out-the-nord-stream

intercepted and recorded Russian radio traffic. The code name of this CIA/NSA mission was "IVY BELLS".[21]

Back to the attack on the Nord Stream pipelines. Here, the first question is who were the accomplices. There are indications that the Swedes were involved, although the Danes should also have been in on it. The fact that, according to Hersh's research, Norway was chosen as an accomplice is perhaps surprising at first glance, but Ivar Strömmen's less plausible explanations fit better into the picture. It seems that Norway was chosen mainly because of their highly qualified divers and their experience in deep-sea operations.

One should not only assume that the Norwegians are loyal to the Nibelung[22] in this project, if that is what happened. Somewhere, there is always something in which the agent of such a project can participate. This is also the case here. If the USA were to succeed with this plan, a new market would suddenly open up for Norwegian gas in Germany. According to Hersh's research, the Norwegians were responsible for finding the right place to plant the explosives on the pipelines. The Norwegians quickly found the right spot, a few kilometres off the coast of Bornholm. There, the two pipelines run at a distance of about 1.5 kilometres from each other, at a depth of about 80 metres. Allegedly, the same US elite diving team that successfully implemented the Ivy Bells project back in 1971 was used to carry out the project. The divers were dropped off by a Norwegian Alta-class mine hunter to place C4 charges on the four pipelines.

---

[21] https://alchetron.com/Operation-Ivy-Bells
[22] a form of unconditional, emotional and potentially fatal fidelity. It goes back to the Middle High German term triuwe, which describes the personal bond in the medieval feudal system.

One of the reasons why the author denied immediately after the attack that the Russians were sabotaging their own pipelines off Bornholm was the aforementioned extremely tight maritime surveillance of the Baltic Sea, which would have had to be circumvented somehow. Obviously, this was also a problem that the alleged American-Norwegian sabotage team had to consider. The solution was to involve the Danes and Swedes, up to a point, in the plan. High-ranking officials on both sides were briefed on possible diving activities in the region. This way, someone higher up could intervene and keep possible reports out of the chain of command, so that the pipeline project remained hidden. "What they were told and what they knew were deliberately two different things," Hersh's source reported. The Norwegian embassy was asked for a statement on this, which has not been forthcoming to date. Apparently, however, there were also problems with the camouflage of the explosive charges, Hersh's secret source reported. It was known that the Russian Navy had surveillance technology capable of detecting and triggering underwater mines. For this reason, an adaptation of the American explosive devices had to be made so that they would appear to be of natural origin on the Russian system. The Norwegians found a solution to this. "This had something to do with adjusting the specific salinity in the water and that in the cargo". They also found a solution to the crucial question of when the operation should take place. The American Sixth Fleet has been organising a large NATO exercise in the Baltic Sea for 21 years, every June, in which numerous allied ships, from all over the region, take part. This exercise is called Baltic Operations 22 or BALTOPS22. The Norwegians were convinced that this would be the ideal cover for the exercise.

The icing on the cake of planning came from the USA. They convinced the planners of the Sixth Fleet to include a research and development exercise in the programme. The exercise involved the Sixth Fleet in collaboration with the US Navy's "Research and Warfare Centres". The exercise, which took place off the coast of Bornholm Island, involved NATO diving teams laying mines while other teams from the exercising forces used the latest underwater technology to find and destroy them. This could have been the perfect cover for the operation, had not Biden, Nuland and others raised so much dust against the pipelines in advance. The divers from Panama City were to do their job and put the C4 explosives in place by the end of BALTOPS22 and put a 48-hour timer on them. All the Americans and Norwegians would have been back in their warm rooms by the time of the first explosion. But nothing is more constant than a change of plan. Washington apparently got cold feet. The time window of 48 hours was now too short for them. So they asked if they could come up with something to remotely detonate the charges at a later time. That way it would not be too obvious that the Americans had a hand in it. The idea was developed that the charges on the pipelines would be triggered by a sonar buoy dropped from an aircraft. The endeavour required the most advanced signal processing technology. Once dropped, the sonar buoy would emit a special sequence of low-frequency tones that would be detected by the remote detonator and, after a preset delay of several hours, detonate the explosives. One problem was that the longer the explosives were stored underwater, the greater the risk that a random signal could set off the charges. According to Hersh's research and according to his source, on 26th September 2022, a Norwegian Navy P8 surveillance aircraft, on what appeared to be a routine flight, dropped said sonar buoy. The signal propagated underwater, first to Nord Stream 2 and then to Nord Stream 1. A few hours later, the high-powered C4 explosive was triggered and three of the four pipelines were destroyed. After a few minutes, the methane gas remaining in the pipes could be seen rising to the surface.

We all know what happened next. Russia was accused by Western leading media and many Western states of having blown up its own pipelines. All this happened without ever having presented even a glimmer of evidence that the Russians were guilty.

When it emerged a few months later that the Russian authorities had been quietly obtaining estimates to repair the pipelines, the theory of who was behind the attack was suddenly no longer so clear. No major Western newspaper addressed the earlier threats against the pipelines made by President Biden and his Secretary of State Nuland. Recently, Victoria Nuland expressed delight at the failure of Nord Stream 2. At a hearing of the Senate Foreign Relations Committee on 26th January 2023, she told Senator Ted Cruz: *"Senator Cruz, like you, I am very pleased, and I think the government is very pleased, that Nord Stream 2 is, as you like to say, just a pile of metal at the bottom of the sea."* [23] Perhaps the new best friend on the continent, Poland, should also have been informed to keep quiet. The tweet by former Polish Foreign Minister and current MEP Radosław Sikorski (EPP Group) was certainly a bit inconvenient for the US, as he seems to have put his finger directly into the wound, or rather into the ruptured pipeline. In conclusion, if the attack on Nord Stream was carried out by the USA, this action against an ally would be an irreparable act of terror that should have consequences. To carry out such an action in view of the fact that millions of people and countless industrial enterprises are dependent on the cheap gas from Russia, which is securely available in the medium term, and that hundreds of thousands of jobs depend on it, is an act of moral baseness that cannot be surpassed.

---

[23] https://www.youtube.com/watch?v=VJdbMj8fStA

So far, Chancellor Olaf Scholz has not dared to address the alleged perpetrator about this aggression or to question him publicly about this event. This act could be interpreted as a declaration of war by the USA against Germany. Unfortunately, the majority still points the finger at the Russians. How naïve do you have to be to believe the stories of the press, the alleged experts and governments who so obviously want to throw you off the scent? No leading politician in Europe, no newspaper and no German news channel has dared to stretch out a finger in the direction of the USA. This is an indictment of supposedly independent journalism. Only two German opposition parties dare to ask questions and demand clarification.[24] [25] Russia introduced a resolution before the UN Security Council on 27th March 2023 calling for an independent investigation into the events surrounding the attack on the pipelines. This received media atten-

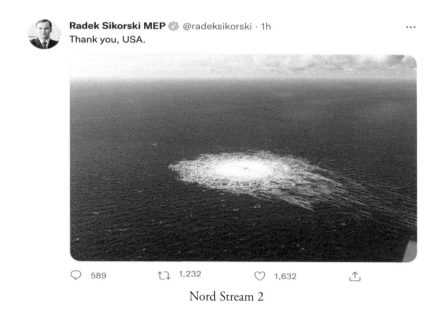

Radek Sikorski MEP ✅ @radeksikorski · 1h
Thank you, USA.

💬 589   🔁 1,232   ♡ 1,632   ↥

Nord Stream 2

[24] https://www.bundestag.de/dokumente/textarchiv/2023/kw11-de-untersuchungsausschuss-nordstream-936464
[25] https://www.bundestag.de/presse/hib/kurzmeldungen-921048

tion, but what the vote and the outcome said about the UN Security Council as an institution was of course not discussed further. Russia failed with its draft resolution calling on the UN to conduct a "comprehensive, transparent and impartial investigation" into the September 2022 attacks. Russia justified this by saying that it had been excluded from the investigations launched by Germany, Denmark and Sweden and that there were accordingly "grave and well-founded doubts"[26] about the objectivity of the national investigations. In the vote on the resolution, Russia received three yes votes (Russia, China, Brazil) for its adoption. 12 states, including the USA, Great Britain, France, Switzerland and Japan, abstained. 12 states thus obviously had no interest whatsoever in a transparent and independent investigation of this terrorist attack, which was obviously perpetrated by one state. With this decision, the UN Security Council discredited itself as an institution and de facto declared itself obsolete. The destruction of three of the four Nord Stream pipes was a geopolitical measure with multiple objectives. Figuratively speaking, spheres of interest of an economic and political nature were shifted "with a crowbar"; new dependencies and forced economic relations were created. At the same time, barriers between states were deepened. The victims of this most reprehensible attack against Germany since the Second World War are Germany and Russia. Germany has supported every sanction up to and including the energy sector. In doing so, it has not only put its good economic relations with Russia at risk, it has ended them, thereby accepting that its own economy and population will suffer damage that is still incalculable. Under increasing pressure from the USA, Germany has made military material available to Ukraine and thus allowed itself to become a stooge in a war that now clearly seems to be turning out to be a half-sided proxy war of the USA with NATO support against Russia on Ukrainian soil. And now there are also many

---

[26] UN Ambassador Vasily Nebensia literally

indications that the USA, possibly also with the support of other states, simultaneously carried out anattack on the energy infrastructure that is essential for Germany.

With all that we have discussed so far, the question that remains un-answered for many is "who is responsible for such a policy"? If we were to condemn the US wholesale for this, we would be making a big mistake. There are many good politicians in the USA who want to pursue a healthy policy of détente, but unfortunately they lack the backing of the lobbying associations and the "think tanks" and non-governmental organisations (NGOs) that are very influential in America. These, in turn, are very closely linked, and just because the president changes does not mean that US foreign policy will change with it. In the next chapter we will take a closer look at who is responsible for current US foreign policy.

The Neocons - Masterminds behind
American Geopolitics

Very often, the term "NEOCONS" is mentioned in connection with American foreign policy. Who or what are these neocons? Where do they come from and what political agenda do they pursue? In general, far too little is known about this. Neocons is the abbreviation for "neoconservat-ives", i.e. the neo or new-conservatives in the USA. This term, however, is extremely misleading, since the neo-cons actually have nothing in com-mon with the classical meaning of conservatism. Nor are they patriots, nor do they have any affinity with such values.

If you look at the exact origins of this movement, none of this is surprising. Neo-cons are liberal globalists, and their firm goal is to make the USA the only dominant world power and to maintain this state at all costs. They are apparently firmly convinced that only the USA is capable of bringing "democracy" to the world; at least this is the image they project to the outside world. States or political forces that stand in the way of this goal are, to put it simply, fought against and, if possible, eliminated through an aggressive foreign policy. The structure from which the neo-cons emerged in the 1960s was called the Liberal Hawks. They were politically liberal-minded individuals who favoured a particularly interventionist policy style in USA foreign policy. They opposed the Cold War, deplored the overly pacifist foreign policy of the Democrats, and were disgusted by the mass pacifist protests against the Vietnam War. Former US Presidents Franklin D. Roosevelt, Harry S. Truman, John F. Kennedy and Lyndon B. Johnson were labelled liberal hawks because they were instrumental in developing the USA into a leading military power. The neo-cons do not define themselves according to any of the American parties. They are neither just Democrats nor Republicans. However, among the liberal hawks in particular, a clear majority are today members of the Democratic Party. Among them Joe Biden, Bill and Hillary Clinton, Madeleine Albright and Zbigniew Brzezinski. In the late 1970s and early 1980s, neo-cons apparently came to the view that liberalism had failed and "no longer knew what it was talking about"[27] The neo-cons quickly abandoned the "liberal" brand. Their policies, the people involved and their pronouncements, however, clearly place the neo-cons in the realm of the globalists. They are convinced representatives of the "New World Order", which, in short, envisages a unipolar world order under the undisputed political, military and

[27] Dionne, E.J.. (1991). Why Americans Hate Politics. New York: Simon & Schuster. pp. 55–61.

economic leadership of the USA. This goal is largely opposed to the national or state self-determination of all other states and important democratic principles also fall victim to this approach, even if the official word is otherwise. In essence, the subordination of states to supranational organisations and non-governmental organisations (NGOs) is being forced through, which in turn are dominated by the USA or the "neo-cons".

Interestingly, some Trotskyists were also among the founders of the neo-cons. Followers of the teachings of the communist mastermind Leon Trotsky[28], who was a strong advocate of internationalism. This in itself is a special phenomenon. Communists are founding a political movement dedicated to globalism, with the purpose of making the USA the sole world power, thus laying the foundations for a somewhat different capitalist-based world revolution. It may seem like a so-called conspiracy theory, but it is more than clear that Left internationalism and liberal capitalist globalism are two sides of the same coin in their orientation. The neo-cons, however, have never tired of railing against communism, which was the original political breeding ground for some of their founders. What blissfully unites the two currents is their quest to put a definitive end to the nation-state principle or to the state-based, democratic self-determination of peoples. The simple desire for state sovereignty, above all nationalism and patriotism, are the declared enemy images of both ideologies.

Neo-cons usually ostensibly advocate the promotion of democracy and are strong advocates of interventionism in international affairs. The definition of democracy, however, is highly dependent on the morals of those who propagate it and for whom it is intended. It has long ceased to be a guarantor of freedom and justice, and the extent to which distorted demo-

---

[28] https://en.wikipedia.org/wiki/Leon_Trotsky

cracy and unbridled interventionism can harmonise with each other is revealed by a look at the USA's double standards, which have even become a state doctrine.

Jeane Kirkpatrick, USA ambassador to the United Nations under President Reagan and a neo-con to the core, wrote about this in a 1979 article in Commentary magazine entitled "Dictatorships and Double Standards". She distinguished between authoritarian regimes and totalitarian regimes such as the Soviet Union. She argued that in some countries' democracy was untenable and that the United States faced a choice between supporting authoritarian governments that could evolve into democracies or Marxist-Leninist regimes that, in her view, never ended once they gained totalitarian control. In such circumstances, it might be wise to ally with authoritarian governments. The only thing that matters in the end is the outcome. In this case: the greatest possible USA political influence on another state. There are many examples of this kind of highly questionable double standard in recent USA history. Whether it was the Carter administration's turning a blind eye to the events in Cambodia, which had to suffer tragically under the communist Khmer Rouge, with the perversity that they were then supported by American arms deliveries via China. The courting of Muammar al-Gaddafi[29] for decades was also evidence of a one-sided, questionable moral concept. George W. Bush was happy to be publicly photographed in the friendliest poses with Hosni Mubarak, the Egyptian President, who in return was accommodating enough to spread more untrue stories about weapons of mass destruction in Iraq. All were strategic allies of American geopolitics and useful stooges for a time. All were used and eventually abandoned/discarded; many of these former allies later be-

---

[29] 1969 to 1979 officially head of state of Libya, ruler until shortly before his death and 2009 to 2010 chairman of the African Union

came enemies or adversaries in wars or proxy wars, instigated civil wars or propaganda campaigns. Despite the facts and clear experiences of the past decades, there are always states that fall for such promises. The following is a brief example to explain the USA approach more vividly:

The so-called Arab Spring swept away both Gaddafi and Mubarak. Some Arab countries suddenly were engulfed in uprisings and civil wars. There were demonstrations for better economic conditions and less totalitarianism, and the USA seized the opportunity not only to support the

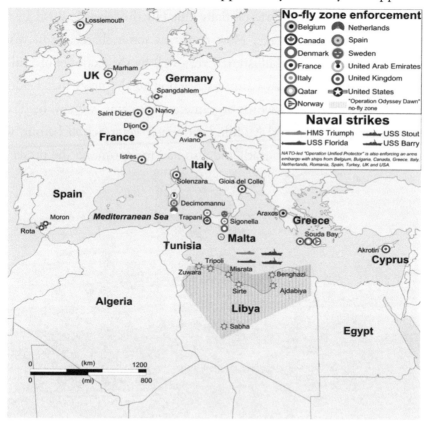

No-fly zone enforcement, Libya

59

insurgents but even to launch this movement. The "coalition of the willing" bombed Libya in the name of justice. NATO, the USA's proxy force, was again involved "out of area" and thus involved in another questionable military operation. The author was able to learn first-hand that participating pilots from Norway were not given clear targets for their bombings.[30] They were instructed to drop their bombs as they saw fit. Without further friend-or-foe reconnaissance, without the reconnaissance of strategic targets.

Muhammar al-Gaddafi was bestially killed by the rebels in 2011 by being impaled alive on a stake. How confused some characters in world politics seem to be can be illustrated very well by the example of Hillary Clinton. The picture shows Clinton's reaction to the news that Gaddafi was dead. Her subsequent words on camera: "We came, we saw, he died". The German journalist and Middle East expert Peter Scholl Latour, was shocked by the manner of death and also had to reprimand the presenter

Clinton's reaction to Gaddafi's death

[30] https://www.nrk.no/dokumentar/libya-piloter-snakker-ut-1.10944493

Sandra Maischberger on German television, who tried to relativise this bestial murder with the argument, "but it is war". If one thing has become obvious in our society, it is that it lacks a necessary measure of morality and ethics. In retrospect, it became known that some ringleaders of the insurgency had participated in programmes of the USA Congress-funded and internationally active institution, the National Endowment for Democracy.[31] The annual grants from the USA budget are part of the State Department's budget. In the 2010 fiscal year, it was 118 million US dollars. In the meantime, this amount has increased to over 300 million US dollars. The main recipients of NED project funds are four foundations that are firmly associated with the organisation and were already involved in its establishment:

The Center for International Private Enterprise (CIPE), affiliated with the US Chamber of Commerce.

The American Center for International Labor Solidarity (ACILS), which is affiliated with the AFL-CIO.

The Democratic Party-affiliated National Democratic Institute for International Affairs (NDI)

The International Republican Institute (IRI), which is affiliated with the Republican Party

Behind this foundation, of course, are other institutions and magazines that promote the same goal and postulate it in an American way. These structures are linked to a not insignificant extent to the neo-cons. It is a

---

[31] https://en.wikipedia.org/wiki/National_Endowment_for_Democracy

prankster's guess that the initial spark for this North African liberation movement, which supposedly arose from within out of discontent, had a different origin. In 2021, two Russian pranksters were able to get leaders of the NED (National Endowment for Democracy) in a video conference to make statements about "modest but significant" support for protests in Russia and Belarus.

It was specifically about the organisations of Alexei Nawalny and Svyatlana Zikhanouskaya.[32] In this context, it is also not surprising that further actions, after the goal was reached, were of no further interest to the US administration. In November 2013, it became known that the Ministry of Justice in Libya was planning to reshape the legal system according to Sharia law. On 4th December 2013, Libya's National Assembly voted in favour of the introduction of Sharia law. The ensuing instability led to a new civil war in Libya, that has been raging since 2014. That was the end of this "spring", which turned into an Arab ice age after the USA lost interest.

The neo-cons first appeared to come to attention with the presidency of George W. "shoot-first-ask-questions-later" Bush, who was himself considered a neo-con and gathered numerous supporters of this movement around him in his leadership. Media in the USA and Europe (often owned by the same small number of internationalist companies) also began to take more notice of the neo-cons and concluded that a major area of their influence was foreign policy and that this was rooted in the Bush Doctrine. Prominent neo-cons include Paul Wolfowitz, Elliott Abrams, Richard Perle and Paul Bremer. Among the high-ranking government officials who

---

[32] http://www.thetimes.co.uk/article/russian-pranksters-trick-us-officials-into-boasting-about-funding-protests-hbtwtvg6n

did not call themselves neo-cons but were very attached to them, were people like former Vice President Dick Cheney and former Secretary of Defence, Donald Rumsfeld. Among the best-known current neo-cons are Robert Kagen and Victoria Nuland, both of whom are also married to each other for convenience.

"We did not go to war in Afghanistan or in Iraq to, quote, ,impose democracy'. We went to war in both places because we saw those regimes as a threat to the United States". ~ Paul Wolfowitz

No intellectual political movement in the USA can do without a think tank. This is also the case with the neo-cons. The Project for the New American Century (PNAC) was a neo-con think tank in Washington, D.C., which focused primarily on U.S.A. foreign policy. It was founded in 1997 by William Kristol and Robert Kagan. PNAC's stated goal was to promote American leadership of the world. For those in charge, it was an incontrovertible view that American leadership is beneficial not only for the USA but also for the entire world.

NATO - From Guarantor of Security to Toothless Tiger?

In the course of what has been discussed so far, a certain scepticism about the North Atlantic defence alliance may have emerged. The apparent dependence on the United States and the consequent lack of independence of the remaining members raise questions. One question, however, overshadows everything else:

To what extent has NATO moved away from the actual purpose of its founding, and is it still contemporary in this constellation? Understanding the NATO construct requires some basic knowledge. Let us first take a look at the period from 1990 onwards. In Russia's view, the West did not stick to the agreement not to expand NATO eastwards following the collapse of communism. To be fair, however, it must be mentioned that there were no written agreements on this. However, a verbal statement was made. This came from Hans-Dietrich Genscher, the then Foreign Minister of the Federal Republic of Germany.

He declared after a consultation with the then American Secretary of State James Baker, in February 1990 in Washington, before an assembled press:

"We agreed that there is no intention of extending the NATO defence area eastwards. That's true, by the way, not only with respect to East Germany, which we don't want to annex, but it's true in general."

In retrospect, however, this statement seems to have been no more than placating lip service after Helmut Kohl, when Chancellor of the Federal Republic of Germany, managed to anger the Soviet Union's Mikhail Gorbachev with his 10-point programme.[33] Gorbachev felt that Kohl was interfering in the internal affairs of the GDR with this programme. At the time, the Soviets were not prepared to agree to the unification of the two German states, the GDR and the FRG. However, Genscher's verbal state-

---

[33] https://ghdi.ghi-dc.org/sub_document.cfm?document_id=223

ment that NATO should not be expanded eastwards made Gorbachev conciliatory again. Vladimir Putin still believes that this promise has not lost its validity and that the West has betrayed Russia by expanding NATO to its borders. Vladimir Polenov, a diplomat who took part in the negotiations in 1990, says today: "It was a mistake not to put down in writing these assurances to the Soviet Union that NATO would not be expanded in the East. That was a very big mistake. Now we have to face the consequences of that mistake." The argumentation in the West is simple: oral commitments have no validity. Hans-Dietrich Genscher formulated only his personal opinion after the meeting with Foreign Minister Baker and the NATO-Russia Founding Act of 1997 clearly shows that Russia has no VETO right in accepting new NATO members. At least that is what can be read on the website "SWR 2 Wissen".[34] The fact that this is not true at all can be quickly proven.

1. Hans Dietrich Genscher made this statement directly after a meeting with Secretary of State James Baker and his staff, to the press in Washington D.C., and the wording was clear. "We agreed..." It did not say, "In my view..." or "I think it is possible to agree...". Apart from that, James Baker repeated this statement to Gorbachev a few days later in Moscow in the presence of the then USA Ambassador Jack Matlock.[35] Matlock commented: "I remember Baker's words":

"You dont have to answer right away, but think about it. Suppose NATO does not extend further east, not an inch: Wouldn't it be better for the future stability of the world if Germany were in NATO, and America continued to have a <u>military presence</u> in Europe?" Gorbachev replied: *"Any NATO expansion to*

[34] https://www.swr.de/wissen/1000-antworten/gab-es-zusagen-an-moskau-die-nato-nicht-nach-osten-zu-erweitern-100.html

[35] https://jackmatlock.com/about/

the east would of course be unacceptable. But I understand what you mean.
And I want to think about it thoroughly." [36] [37]

2. The NATO-Russia Founding Act states the following in connection with a right of VETO:

"The provisions of these Acts shall not in any respect give NATO or Russia veto power over each other's actions, nor impair or limit the rights of NATO or Russia to independent decision-making and action. They may not serve as a means to interfere with the interests of other states."

This indeed leaves much room for interpretation. One thing, however, is clear. There is not a word about accepting new members into NATO in this passage. Nor does "independent decision-making and independent action" automatically implement Russia's agreement to renounce or the right to indifference on the part of NATO or the USA to its commitment, whether made orally or in writing. The Founding Act can be read to mean that every state has the right to apply for membership of NATO. No one wants to question this right, because it is a process of decision-making by sovereign states. But this is not inevitably synonymous with agreeing to admit every one of these states. Of course, this is only in the light of what has been said at the highest political level. NATO and the USA could well have decided against the membership of the former Warsaw Pact member states based on the commitment made and the agreements under the Founding Act, with the focus on friendship and cooperation. This might have resulted in a separate structure of these states, which would have been <u>organised as a </u>result of the rejection. In accordance with the formulated

[36] https://www.mdr.de/geschichte/zeitgeschichte-gegenwart/politik-gesellschaft/zwei-plus-vier-verhandlungen-deutsche-einheit-nato-osterweiterung-putin-100.html
[37] https://books.openedition.org/ceup/2906?lang=de

wish of the NATO-Russia Founding Act, for a more transparent approach for both sides and more willingness to cooperate, such behaviour with regard to eastward enlargement would with the greatest possible certainty have caused less irritation on the Russian side and less concern. The Founding Act itself takes a clear position on this several times.

"In the course of strengthening the OSCE, NATO and Russia will work together to exclude any possibility of a return to a Europe of division and confrontation or isolation of any state". "The main task of this Permanent Joint Council will be to build ever greater confidence, formulate unified goals and develop the practice of permanent consultation and co-operation between NATO and Russia in order to enhance each other's security and that of all states in the Euro-Atlantic area without compromising the security of any state".

Finally, it should be noted that the term "new members" is used once in the entire Founding Act. The following is the line of text:

"NATO member states reiterate that they have no intention, no plans, and no reason to deploy nuclear weapons on the territory of new members, nor do they see any need to change NATO's nuclear posture or policy in any respect - nor do they see any need to do so in the future".

Again, this leaves room for interpretation: Albania, Northern Macedonia, Montenegro, Croatia, are all new member states that joined after the signing of the Founding Act. This kind of NATO enlargement would probably not even have elicited a shrug of the shoulders from Russia, especially if the agreements for transparency and understanding with Russia had been adhered to. The possibilities were there, everything is there in black and white. So why didn't they seek dialogue with Russia instead of presenting it with a fait accompli? NATO's enlargement to the East contradicts at least to what was said in 1990 by Hans-Dietrich Genscher and the American Secretary of State James Baker. Such word-breaking behaviour may be possible as a private person in the neighbourhood and one might get away with it unchallenged, but at an international political level and with states that once stood opposite each other as enemies and have the largest arsenals of weapons in the world, including nuclear weapons, such behaviour must be described as utterly foolish. It cannot be denied that the suspicion arises that the statement made and the NATO-Russia Founding Act were merely intended to buy time vis-à-vis Russia for their own expansionist plans. In view of the fact that admission processes take a certain amount of time, one must assume that the first talks and plans on the part of the USA or the NATO leadership must have begun in the mid-1990s. The Russian army had possibly not even been withdrawn from the GDR as agreed and the NATO-Russia Founding Act had not even been signed when preparations for NATO's eastward expansion were presumably already underway. In the USA, however, there are also politicians with great integrity who warned early on against an eastward expansion of NATO. At least an expansion that would clearly extend into Russia's sphere of interest. Three of these far-sighted individuals are quoted below:

Pat Buchanan, former White House communications director under Ronald Reagan, journalist and TV commentator wrote in his 1999 book "a republic, not an empire":

"By moving NATO to Russia's doorstep, we have planned a twenty-first century confrontation".

Robert Gates, director of the CIA for 26 years and then USA Secretary of Defence under Bush Jr. and Obama until 2011, also wrote in his 2015 memoirs:

"It was a mistake to act so quickly [NATO enlargement]. Trying to bring Georgia and Ukraine into NATO was a real overreach and a particularly monumental provocation."

Jack Matlock Jr, a USA diplomat in the Soviet Union from 1987 – 1991, mentioned earlier in this chapter, warned in 1997 that NATO enlargement...

was *"the greatest strategic mistake"* and *"could foster a chain of events that could lead to the greatest security threat since the collapse of the Soviet Union".*

We have now read some of the arguments that Russia had a right to regard NATO's actions as "Неприятный" (unpleasant). However, since this book is by no means intended to favour one side or the other, let us now consider the question of what would have happened if the countries of the former Warsaw Pact had not had the opportunity to join NATO? As an example, let us take a look at the Baltic states. In all the states of the Baltics, as in Ukraine, there were aspirations for independence after the collapse of the Soviet Union. Without pre-empting the chapter on the Baltic States, there were deaths in the quest for independence as a result of Russian attempts to put down these movements in all the Baltic States. The Baltics will never forget the period of Soviet oppression, the struggles for their freedom and for their right to self-determination. The fear of being occupied by Russia again runs deep, not only in the Baltic States. This understandable concern is ultimately what drove the Warsaw Pact countries into the arms of NATO. Never again Russian paternalism, never again communism were the all-important slogans, and precisely as far as communism was concerned, Russia did not cut a good figure in the years from 1993 to 1999. The Communist Party's election results rose from election to election. In 1993 it had 12.4 per cent of the vote, but by 1995 it had 22.3 per cent, making it the strongest single party in the country. In the 1996 presidential elections, Boris Yeltsin's lead over Gennady Zyuganov[38] was only 3%. In 1999, the election result was increased again to 24.3 per cent. The ultra-nationalists under Vladimir Zhirinovsky were another party that contributed to the overall impression that Russia was not developing into the democracy hoped for by the West. Given these figures, the concerns of the immediate neighbours are eminently understandable. The danger that Russia, after a period of economic and military recovery, might again feel compelled to annex its smaller neighbours must be taken as a given. Russia's current policy, which certainly shows imperialist tendencies that have been increasingly evident for some years, as well as the renewed glorification of the Soviet Union, leaves no doubt that the sovereignty of Russia's immediate neighbours cannot be regarded as being endangered even at the present time without good reason. It should also be borne in mind that Russian President Putin is now more of a balancing, moderate force in Russia's political landscape, while increasingly nationalist and extreme forces with harsh rhetoric, such as Dmitri Anatoljewitsch Medwedew, former president of the Russian Federation, seem to be gaining the upper hand.

It is easy from a neutral and non-threatened position, such as that of Germany, to recognise a breach of a commitment made between the USA,

---

[38] A Russian politician and has been Chairman of the Central Committee of the Communist Party of the Russian Federation since 14 February 1993.

Germany and Russia and to condemn the eastward expansion of NATO as aggressive geopolitics. However, a healthy assessment always includes taking into account the views and sensitivities of all parties or states concerned, and it is precisely that of the former Soviet satellite states that the pro-Russian forces like to sweep under the carpet. It should be clear that one does not make friends in Eastern Europe with this one-sided political view. We, those not directly affected, should therefore ask ourselves, what right we have to want to take one side or the other without the participation of all Eastern European peoples and taking their opinions into account. In the rarest of cases, we actually have all the necessary information at our fingertips.

But now back to the actual topic. The eastward expansion of NATO, criticised by the Russians, began in 1999 with Poland, the Czech Republic and Hungary. This was the starting signal for the preparations for a flood of countries from the former Eastern Bloc, unimaginable since the founding of NATO in 1949. In 2004, Bulgaria, Estonia, Latvia, Lithuania, Slovenia and Slovakia joined NATO. That this former adversary, which is in fact controlled by the USA, was now suddenly on their own doorstep as a result of the enlargement was undoubtedly perceived by the the Russian Federation as a potential threat to their own spheres of interest. In this context, we must not forget that it was the USA that unilaterally terminated the ABM Treaty of 1972 in December 2001. In principle, this treaty ensured the balance of power, the status quo, by contractually limiting missile defence systems for intercontinental ballistic missiles. In 2004, the USA announced its intention to station a first missile defence system for intercontinental ballistic missiles in Alaska. In August 2006, it was reported that the USA wanted to protect Europe with a newly developed missile defence shield. Against whom? was the first question, and the official answer was more than implausible: the USA allegedly wanted to protect Europe and itself from missiles from Iran[39], the USA's great bogeyman, protection from missiles which, incidentally, Iran does not possess to this day! Initially, there was even talk of a threat from North Korea, at least until the "experts" took a look at the globe and realised that North Korea would certainly not fire its missiles in that direction at America.[40] So against whom was this missile defence shield really aimed at? If we look at where this missile defence was built, the answer is readily available. Originally, Poland and the Czech Republic were planned as sites. Then in 2009, the then USA President Barack Obama decided not to build the radar installation in the Czech Republic. A better place was found where the population apparently had less antipathy towards the installation of such a system by the Americans: Romania, in this case. Interesting in this context is the fact that the USA carried out its strategic arrangements without consulting its NATO "partners", especially France and Germany. This completely arrogant behaviour could well have been interpreted as a violation, if not a breach, of the transatlantic link. However, there was no reaction from the Europeans and once again they demonstrated their shameful submission to the transatlantic hegemony.

A year earlier, in 2008, the NATO summit took place in Bucharest. After NATO's eastward enlargement had come to an end four years earlier, the cat was now let out of the bag. President Barack Obama announced at the summit that Georgia and Ukraine would be admitted to NATO under any circumstances. At this point it had become obvious to the Russians that a strategic cooperation of the West with Russia on the basis of the

---

[39] https://www.reuters.com/article/us-bush-shield-idUSWAT00833920071023

[40] https://www.spiegel.de/politik/ausland/geheimstudien-stellen-geplanten-us-raketenabwehr-schirm-in-frage-a-882371.html

NATO-Russia Founding Act[41] was obviously not desired at all. From a rational point of view, it is inexplicable why a state like Georgia should be accepted into NATO. Geographically, it belongs to the Near East and, at least at first glance, has no geopolitical or military-strategic relevance. A different picture emerges, however, if one assumes that the USA, with the help of NATO, intends to encircle Russia or to establish itself in these peripheral regions in the long term. The question of the actual motivation, however, will be addressed in one of the following chapters.

Let's shed some more light on NATO and take a more concrete look at the founding years. Here, too, we can already see some clear indications of how USA geo-strategy exhibits a certain pattern. Before NATO was founded in 1949, there was a predecessor organisation made up of the former anti-Hitler coalition. Initially, this consisted only of France and Great Britain, both of which laid the foundation for further development with the Dunkirk Agreement in 1947. With the Brussels Pact of 17th March 1948, the Netherlands, Belgium and Luxembourg joined this agreement, which from then on was directed towards collective self-defence against any armed attack in Europe on one of its members. Originally, the main aim was to be able to completely exclude Germany as a potential threat. This structure was not yet the North Atlantic Treaty! The United States of America demanded only a few months later that any European state that wanted to be defended by the USA would also have to defend America in the event of an attack. The developments of 1948/49 brought into focus in Western Europe a possible military threat from the communist Eastern Bloc, led by the Soviet Union. The Western European states therefore turned to the USA for military assistance against possible Soviet aggression. The USA used this request to establish the North Atlantic Treaty Or-

---

[41] https://www.nato.int/cps/en/natohq/official_texts_25468.htm?selectedLocale=en

ganisation and thereby secure continued legitimacy to remain militarily in Europe. The first strategic concept for the defence of the North Atlantic area was drawn up from 1st December 1949 and approved by the North Atlantic Council as early as 6th January 1950. It was based on the USA strategy of "containment". The principle was to stop the defence against a Soviet attack on the Alliance area as far east as possible. In 1952, the first eastward enlargement of NATO took place with the accession of Greece and Turkey. This created the first direct border between the Soviet Union and NATO territory. With the signing of the Paris Treaties, on 23rd October 1954, the Federal Republic of Germany was invited (or told) to join, thus completing a strategically important step in the FRG's integration into the West by incorporating it into the NATO zone of influence.

In fact, there was no reason for the FRG to join. Protection against a Soviet attack appears to be a pretext, since three large Western armies were already then permanently stationed on the territory of the FRG. The Soviet Union would certainly not have risked a confrontation of this kind. A neutral position, as in the case of Austria, would undoubtedly have been the better choice for the Federal Republic of Germany. That this would even have been advocated by the Soviet Union is proven by the note from Stalin to the USA, Great Britain and France sent on 10th March 1952 by the deputy Soviet foreign minister Andrei Gromyko. In it, he proposed a united, sovereign, democratic Germany. It should be allowed to have a limited army, but in return it should maintain neutrality. Based on this proposal, a peace treaty was then to be negotiated with an all-German government. The Western powers rejected this proposal.

On 16th March 1955, US President Dwight D. Eisenhower announced the use of tactical nuclear weapons against military targets in the event of war. Despite the FRG's NATO membership, it was obvious to many in which area the so-called strategy of containing a Soviet attack would take place. The GDR and the FRG were supposed to serve as nuclear buffer zones. For decades, our own government has been selling us Germans how important and correct all these processes were in order to guarantee German interests and German security. Unfortunately, they fail to admit that then, as now, it was not really about German interests. The restoration of German unity, the end of the occupation by the Allies and the establishment of territorial integrity as well as the attainment of full sovereignty should have been the highest priority of a German foreign policy, but this was lost sight of at the latest since the 1970s and the Western Allies did not seem to care much about a united Germany.

It was not until later that year, on 14th May 1955 and thus a good five years after the founding of NATO, that the Warsaw Pact was founded as a counterweight to NATO, particularly because of the FRG's accession to NATO and Eisenhower's announcement on the use of nuclear weapons. Until then, the Eastern Bloc states had only been united in an economic community, the "Council for Mutual Economic Assistance".

The Americans had already assumed the leading role in NATO's command structure at that time, and an essential purpose of NATO became increasingly apparent. The premise was to keep the US militarily, economically and politically constant in Europe, to keep Russia out and keep Germany down. This was formulated by the British peer, Lord Ismay, first NATO Secretary General, who was convinced that his political career was built on this very statement.[42]

---

[42] https://www.nato.int/cps/en/natohq/declassified_137930.htm

Since its foundation, NATO has been an institution supposedly limited in its radius of action to the North Atlantic - European area. The defence of the members of the North Atlantic Treaty was the sole reason for NATO's existence. Later on, the influence of the USA on NATO's policy became more and more pronounced, and it was also misused for the implementation of USA geopolitical goals through targeted interventions. Thus, in recent years, NATO has increasingly been shown to be a military tool of the USA. One of the "new ideas" is NATO's readiness for "out-of-area" missions, which was agreed in 1992. With the authorisation of the UN Security Council or the OSCE, missions outside NATO territory should thus also be possible. As a result, NATO did not shy away from breaking international law, as in the case of its active participation in the war in Yugoslavia, where it even renounced a UN mandate and thus became a party to the war itself. NATO's air strikes during the Kosovo war are still highly controversial today. They were not above creating false information in order to justify wars. We know this at the latest since Colin Powell's[43] little "anthrax fib", the non-existent weapons of mass destruction in Iraq or, just now, the alleged protection of Europe from missiles from Iran and Korea. Colin Powell later described this appearance before the UN Security Council as a blot on his career. Let's take a look at a few facts and figures. The Alliance currently consists of 30 states. Its headquarters are in Brussels. In 2018, it moved into a new building there, which cost around 1.2 billion euros. Why many experts describe NATO as a sluggish bureaucratic monster becomes clear when one takes a closer look at the political institutions and command structures.

First, there is the North Atlantic Council, NATO's most important political decision-making body. Each member state has a seat on the North

---

[43] Secretary of State of the United States (2001-2005)

Atlantic Council (NAC). It meets at least once a week or as needed at different levels. This is followed by the Nuclear Planning Group (NPG). This is the member body responsible for the role of nuclear weapons in NATO. The so-called "High-Level Group (HLG)", led by the USA, acts within it. In this group, among other things, the foundations were laid for the NATO Double-Track-Decision,[44] which is still controversial today. In addition, there are other civilian and military groups, boards, committees and sub-committees, which cannot all be mentioned here in detail. In addition, there is the Euro-Atlantic Partnership Council, the NATO-Russia Council, the NATO-Georgia Committee and the NATO-Ukraine Committee.

The military command structure is composed as follows:

Strategic level
ACO - Allied command Operation
ACT - Allied command Transformation

Operational level
JFC - Joint Force Command Brunsum
JFC - Joint Force Command Naples
JFC - Joint Force Command Norfolk

Tactical Level
MARCOM - Maritime Command, Northwood
AIRCOM - Air Command, Ramstein
LANDCOM - Land Command, Izmir

---

[44] https://en.wikipedia.org/wiki/NATO_Double-Track_Decision

Support Command
JSEC - Joint Support and Enabling Command, Ulm

The entire structure presented here is solely for administrative purposes, as well as for military-strategic planning. Since 2021, Germany has been paying an annual community contribution of over 400 million euros to NATO. Incidentally, this is more or less the same as the USA, which recently pushed through a reduction of its share by 120 million euros. In 2022, the total was 446 million euros. In 2023, Germany is to pay another 90 million euros more into the Alliance's coffers. This is justified by the massive increase in NATO's overall budget, which has been increased from 2.5 billion euros in 2022, to 3.32 billion euros in 2023. This finances the alliance headquarters in Brussels and the military headquarters, as shown above. As an institution, NATO has no military units of its own. These are provided by the Allies when needed and, as we will see in a moment, are also deployed at their own discretion. This leads us directly to the essential question: What actually happens in an emergency? Most states promise themselves support from their allies in the event of an attack on their own territory. Article 5 of the NATO Treaty is often invoked. But this article leaves room for speculation, as we will see below. The original text states:

"The Parties agree that an armed attack against one or more of them in Europe or North America shall be considered an attack against them all and consequently they agree that, if such an armed attack occurs, each of them, in exercise of the right of individual or collective self-defense recognized by Article 51 of the Charter of the United Nations, will assist the Party or Parties so attacked by taking henceforth, individually and in concert with the other Parties, such action as it deems necessary, including the use of armed force, to restore and maintain the security of the North Atlantic area."

Essentially, only four words of the penultimate line matter. "as it deems necessary". This is decided by each member state absolutely individually. There is therefore explicitly no obligation to use armed force in response to an attack by a third state on an Ally. Supportive and humanitarian services would also be sufficient within the framework of an individual assessment. That NATO obviously likes to make promises when it comes to acquiring new members was very clearly demonstrated in Bucharest in 2008. The outbreak of the Ukraine war has breathed some life back into the ailing alliance and, in a way, given it a reprieve if not a renaissance. But this cannot hide the fact that the European nations need a European alternative to NATO that is independent of global, non-European interests in order not to become a permanent pawn in the game of foreign geopolitical objectives. Especially in view of the hopes that countries like Estonia, Latvia and Lithuania in particular place in NATO, and now Finland has joined and Sweden is considering joining. They want to join solely on the basis of a hoped-for guaranteed protection. It is all the more worrying that this assistance is de facto only an optional extra. The responses of a British NATO officer to a direct question from the Estonian Prime Minister on how NATO would react to a Russian attack on Estonia was highly revealing. The answer was that they would first withdraw to the depths of Europe to assess the situation and then regain the territory later.[45] When asked how long this might take, the answer was: about one to two months. With the sober realisation that by then, in the event of a Russian attack, as unlikely as it seems at present, there would be nothing left of Estonia or any of the other Baltic states to defend, the disillusionment was certainly great.

---

[45] https://www.lrt.lt/en/news-in-english/19/1725924/estonian-pm-says-baltic-states-would-be-wiped-off-the-map-under-current-nato-plans

The Drive to the East - What Drives the USA?

The USA sees itself as the last remaining world power, the only one empowered and capable of bringing the light of "democracy" over the dark spots of the world.

"Only American power can hold the natural forces of history at bay" [46]
Robert Kagan

The geostrategic planning for these ostensible goals, behind whichof course lies something else, is based on long-term objectives. It was realised very early on, that certain goals cannot be realised within a few years. The implementation of some of these geopolitical upheaval processes can also take decades or even longer. What is less overt in all that is known so far, is the theory underlying these plans. If we look at how vehemently the USA entrenched itself in Europe after the Second World War, we might assume that the reason was in fact the alleged protection of Europe from a Soviet threat; but on closer examination this was only a means to an end, for the permanent retention of the USA in Europe was an essential component of US strategy.

---

[46] https://www.foreignaffairs.com/united-states/robert-kagan-free-world-if-you-can-keep-it-ukraine-america?utm_medium=newsletters&utm_source=twofa&utm_campaign=Putin%E2%80%99s%20Last%20Stand&utm_content=20221223&utm_term=-FA%20This%20Week%20-%20112017

"For America, the most important geopolitical prize is Eurasia.... Now a non-Eurasian power is dominant in Eurasia - and America's global supremacy depends directly on how long and how effectively its domination of the Eurasian continent is maintained." Zbigniew Brzeziński, "The grand Chessboard"

After the fall of the Iron Curtain, the USA could have reduced its troop presence in Europe to a minimum or done the same as the Russians and ended it completely. In fact, the plan envisaged something different. The presence of US troops in Europe was gradually reduced from 265,000 soldiers in 1990 to the current 100,000. At first glance, this is quite a significant reduction in troop strength. At second glance, however, it becomes clear that the US calculation was more like a shell game. NATO as an institution is, as we know, the elementary pillar of the US presence in Europe. Strengthening NATO and expanding it accordingly was and is thus a priority goal of the US. If one can now reduce one's own costs at the same time, this is the proverbial killing of two birds with one stone. This is what has happened by announcing and implementing a reduction of US troops and at the same time consistently working on the admission of all former Eastern bloc countries into the NATO alliance. The number of soldiers gained through NATO's eastward enlargement amounts to 352,000. If we now subtract the withdrawn US troops, we are left with a plus of 187,300 soldiers and military equipment for NATO.

As we know, the eastward enlargement was followed by provocations such as the promise of NATO membership to Ukraine and Georgia as well as the construction of a missile defence shield, obviously directed against Russia. It has now turned out that it can also be used offensively and is capable of firing land-based Tomahawk missiles. These missiles can be equipped with nuclear warheads with an explosive power of 5 to 150 KT.

These launching systems are now located in Poland and Romania. Whether the possibility of equipping them with nuclear weapons violates the agreement made in the NATO-Russia Founding Act, not to station nuclear weapons in the countries of new members, is certainly a matter of sufficient debate. Let's take a look at the number and position of US military bases in the world for orientation. The encirclement of Russia and China is very obvious. Neither Russia nor China have anywhere near as many military bases in the world and neither of them is trying to press the US militarily in any way, for example with Russian military bases in Central America. Russia has about 25 bases outside its borders in 9 different countries, all former Soviet republics. Syria is the only exception. China has a single base outside its own territory in the former French colony of Djibouti on the Horn of Africa. The USA, on the other hand, has 750 military bases worldwide. This imbalance almost invites the USA to override the interests of other countries. What is the USA aiming at with this

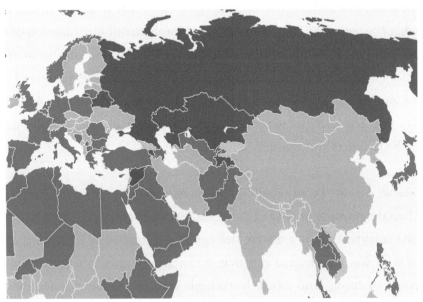

Blue = USA bases. Red = Russian bases. Green = USA + RUS

behaviour and what is the reason for it? Polemically, one could now claim that the USA is trying to seize world domination.

As polemical as this may sound at first glance, it is not quite so wrong, as explained in more detail below. The turn of the 19th and 20th centuries is considered the official beginning of modern geopolitical thinking and theories. The origins must be seen in the worldwide policies of discovery, conquest, trade and colonialism pursued by the British (later the British Empire), the French, Belgians, Dutch, Spanish and Portuguese. We had already learned earlier, that Germany and Sweden were in some ways the pioneers of modern geopolitics. Now, however, we come to the gentleman whose name was already mentioned: the Briton Sir John Halford Mackinder (1861-1947), a geographer who later devoted himself to economics and political science. He was a corrector in geography at the University of Oxford, which was the highest possible position for a British geographer. He was a co-founder of the University of Reading and the London School for Economics. In 1902 he wrote his first work on the geo-morphology of the British Isles. In a sense, it could be called the preliminary to his subsequent work, which remains one of the most important works in the world of geopolitics. His essay "The Geographical Pivot of History" was first presented to the Royal Geographical Society and later became part of his work "Democratic ideals and reality". With this work he established the so-called Heartland Theory. Mackinder, of course, looked at geopolitics through the eyes of a Briton and from the perspective of one of the leading naval and world power of his time. He formulated this theory as a warning to his countrymen, and especially to the rulers of his country, that with the advance of technological development, supremacy as a maritime power would deteriorate vis-à-vis the continental powers. In his work, he took a comparative view of land and sea powers. He included in his work factors such as geographical location, raw material deposits, population resources, industry, technical progress and economic development. His theory is based on the materialistic view of a man of the 20th century, which has not changed much in geopolitical considerations to this day. Men strive for security and prosperity within the framework of their needs. We are in constant competition with others for territory and resources. Until the advent of rapid technological progress, Mackinder saw naval powers as superior to continental powers. He argued that both maritime and continental powers have always acted as factors influencing history. Britain's effective control of the world's oceans provided the kingdom with a hegemonic position well into the 20th century. It was thus always able to assert itself against expanding continental powers, which seized naval bases from the land side and were thus able to defeat even larger naval powers. According to Mackinder, Britain lost this position through modern inventions such as the steam engine, railways and the internal combustion engine, which ensured that continental powers could massively expand and accelerate their transport routes. After the end of the First World War, he revised his theory once again, producing what is probably the most important geopolitical theory to date.

In it, Mackinder divides the surface of the world into the following subareas:

The world island:
It consists of the contiguous continents of Europe, Asia and Africa. It is the richest, largest and most populous of all possible connections of countries.

The coastal islands:

Islands arranged in a crescent shape around the world island. They include the United Kingdom.

The offshore islands:
Also arranged in a crescent shape around the offshore islands. They include the double continents of the Americas, Australia, and Japan.

At the centre of all these is the so-called Heartland. It stretches from the Volga to the Yangtze and from the Himalayas to the Arctic. If we look at the map, we can see very clearly which country we are essentially dealing with here: Russia.

If the heartland of the Eurasian continent, i.e. Western Siberia and the European part of Russia, had a similarly well-developed transport network as the

Sir John Halford Mackinder

industrialised countries of Western Europe and, as a result, a high degree of industrialisation as well as an equally high degree of economic penetration, this country would be able to exercise enormous power. It would be one of the most powerful continental states, or possibly the most powerful continental state, which could exert a great influence on the surrounding islands and would probably sooner or later take over the rule of the world island.

Mackinder formulated three memorable maxims in this regard:

"He who rules over Eastern Europe rules over the Heartland."

"Whoever rules over the Heartland rules over the World Island."

"He who rules the world island rules the world."

Domination of the Heartland, according to Mackinder, would result in a continuously growing influence on the continental Rimlands and eventually on the American double continents, Australia and Japan. Influenced by the lessons of the First World War, Mackinder speculated that if Germany had been able to concentrate all its strength on dominating the East, it could have brought the world island under its control from there. The naval powers would then have already been largely deprived of their naval bases, as described above. He was convinced that the Atlantic powers had

THE NATURAL SEATS OF POWER.
Pivot area—wholly continental. Outer crescent—wholly oceanic. Inner crescent—partly continental, partly oceanic.

The world map according to Mackinder's theory

only narrowly escaped this danger. Mackinder's theory has often been the starting point of controversial discussions ever since. The geopolitical considerations of the German Karl Haushofer in the 1930s, which soon led to the theory of "Lebensraum" in the East, were also based on Mackinder's theory.

Shortly before the USA entered the Second World War, the American geologist Nicholas J. Spykman (1893 - 1943) began to study the theory and adapted it to US interests. Spykman was a Dutch-American geostrategist. He was the intellectual originator of the USA containment policy, which we have read about before in connection with NATO's first defence concept. Spykman was a political scientist and co-founder of the realist school of international politics.[47] As a professor of international relations, he taught at Yale University. One of his main concerns was to teach his students the importance of geography: Geopolitics could only be understood with the help of geography. As already mentioned, Spykman modified the Heartland Theory and essentially turned it into the Rimland Theory. The main difference with Mackinder's theory is the assumption that the power of the heartland can be contained and controlled by dominating the surrounding rimlands. Spykman believed that isolationism, i.e. retreating into one's own hemisphere and at the same time dominating the world's oceans, could not protect the USA effectively enough. He was convinced that it was

Nicholas J. Spykman

[47] Realism, is a school of thought within the political science discipline of International Relations that deals with the character and distribution of power in the international system.

essential to prevent the USA's withdrawal from Europe after the Second World War and not to repeat the mistake of the First World War. In his book, "The Geography of Peace", which was published only a year after his death, the most important approach in his view was that the balance of power in Eurasia also directly affected the security of the USA.

In his writings on geography and foreign policy, he follows deterministic ideas. Since geography was "the most fundamental factor because of its permanence", the potential foreign policy of a state had to be analysed mainly on the basis of its geographical circumstances. Spykman argued that it would have been important for Germany to continue to have a strong influence in Europe after the end of the war in order to balance Russia's power in Europe. However, according to his theory, there was no difference between Germany having influence as far as the Urals and Russia having influence as far as Germany. According to Spykman, both variants were a threatening scenario for the USA. Since Germany was no longer a counterweight to Russia after the war and no other power in Europe had the necessary potential to fill this role, the obvious consequence was to find a legitimate reason to anchor the USA in Europe in the long term, which would secure the security and supremacy of the USA. Spykman predicted the defeat of Japan. China and Russia would also come into conflict sooner and later because of border disputes. China is already pushing this conflict in schools, where children are already being taught parts of Siberia with Chinese names and some areas are being portrayed as lost territories that would one day belong to China again. Spykman also predicted the rise of China as an Asian superpower. For this reason, the USA would have to take over the "defence" of Japan, since otherwise China would sooner or later annex this territory. Even then, Spykman did not think much of European integration. A balance of power in Europe would be more advantageous for America than a unified structure. According to Spykman, the war against Germany was fought to prevent the conquest of Europe. A federalisation of Europe would be against the interests of the USA because the war was fought to maintain a balance of power in Europe.

This is further proof, that the European Union is only allowed to exist because it only has a superficial federalised appearance. But as Zbigniew Brzeziński said, it does not speak with one voice and disagrees internally on many things and thus does not pose a real threat to the USA. Zbigniew Brzeziński, but also influential politicians in the USA such as Henry Kissinger, have been strongly influenced in their work by this theory and the considerations derived from it. The behaviour of the USA over the last 100 years seems more coherent in the context of this theory. The constant drive to the east, to the Eurasian peripheries (Rimland), far from its territory, is rather an urge to consolidate the USA's own ultimate supremacy, which can only be achieved by controlling these territories. As long as another power has the means to use the resources available there to the disadvantage of the USA, a lasting safeguarding of its own interests in this geographical region is at great risk. Critics may feel obliged to counter that an open confrontation between the USA and Russia is still unlikely. The author does not want to contradict this at all, but the capture of a country can also be done very effectively by more subtle means. Waging proxy wars is a common way for the USA to achieve its own goals without having to justify itself as directly responsible. The replacement of governments through infiltration, support of opposition groups, influential structures and persons is, as we have already experienced, an opportune means to achieve the geopolitical goals of the USA.

Other great powers use different methods: large economic investments, buying up energy suppliers and other infrastructure companies such as ports and securing long-term supply contracts are, among other things, very effective geo-political tools that China uses and which, as the development of the country shows, can also be regarded as effective. This method, however, requires special economic preconditions that can now be found neither in the USA nor in Europe. China's influence in Africa has grown steadily in recent years and it has also long since begun to expand its spheres of influence in Europe in this way.

The current situation in Eastern Europe

The fall of the Soviet Union set in motion many things that were previously thought to be set in stone for eternity. One by one, the former Soviet republics declared themselves independent. The urge for freedom, democracy and self-determination had become insatiable after a good five decades of communist paternalism and suppression of their own culture. It was similar for the people in the former GDR. The political and economic drive towards the West and the seemingly endless opportunities it offered was tantamount to a once-in-a-lifetime chance. However, as great as people's joy was they were naive about the West. They believed they would encounter a similar socialisation, a similar solidarity with one another, and had not reckoned with jumping headfirst into a capitalist shark tank. Superficiality, disinterest, hostility, competitiveness and often deceit and betrayal or intrigue as methods were things one did not know or expect from one's own habitat. The path of the new governments in Eastern Europe was paved with good intentions and they all brought with them a certain hunger for influence, greed for money, and opportunity. The seemingly collective quest for freedom and democracy was understandable and crucial to later developments. The USA stood at the ready and brought "freedom and democracy - made in the USA" to the states in Eastern Europe. With NATO membership, protection from Russia was assured and a few well-fed economic bosses were brought along to influence the local economy in the long term, off course in the interests of the USA and USA companies.

The eastward enlargement of the EU was a real (financial) blessing for every new member state. None of the new member states had to do or prove much to be accepted into the community. The billions of euros in subsidies flowed sustainably. EU enlargement to the East was not a major problem for the newly formed Russian Federation under Boris Yeltsin in the 1990s, at least not until the current state of affairs. Especially since Yeltsin was a loyal vassal of the USA leadership and gradually robbed himself of his sanity through increasing alcohol consumption. On the one hand, both the Russian and the US side were aware of the shortcomings of the EU. On the other hand, it could have been worthwhile for the Russian economy to co-operate economically in certain areas. NATO's eastward enlargement and the expansion of the USA missile defence shield were of a completely different quality. It was obvious that it was about the creation and expansion of spheres of interest. The Russians observed the development extremely passively, without themselves taking care to improve relations with their immediate neighbours. In the last 10 years, one could also observe a clear change in Russian rhetoric. With regard to history and the Soviet Union, a certain transfiguration has reappeared among

Russians, which can be seen as extremely disconcerting and should be a negative sign for all those who are not categorically hostile to Russia. Comments and formulations such as "The Soviet Union was not so bad after all" and "the people were doing well", "nobody was oppressed" were heard by the author himself from a Russian lady at a reception of the German Parliamentary Society. The reference to the oppression of other cultures, right down to the language, or the deportations to gulags, was dismissed by her as stupid! Thank God, this is not the view of all Russians, but a disturbing tendency can be heard that could severely impair peaceful co-existence with European neighbours in the future if a rational view of factual history does not take hold here again. Incidentally, it is a good example of Russia's central problem. A creeping defiance of rejection, mistrust of Russia and a lack of self-critical understanding that far-reaching foreign policy difficulties might also be rooted in its own behaviour.

A lack of communication with its immediate Eastern European neighbours, the former Soviet republics, can be seen as one of the biggest failures for years. This very important communication from the Russian side should have been cultivated on an equal footing and free from the influence of the USA, which has proven to have little interest in constructive dialogue and agreement in this direction. The strong and multi-layered geopolitical influence of the USA and the unwillingness of the Russians to take the initiative in communicating with their neighbours in order to cultivate a relationship of trust and, on the other hand, the still enormous credulity of the still young democracies, but also recently Finland and Sweden, with regard to promises from the West, are factors that have made the current situation in Eastern Europe possible in the first place. An exception to the last point is Hungary, which has largely protected itself from outside influences in various ways through domestic policy measures. The

USA, Poland and Lithuania should stop encouraging the Ukrainian leadership to continue the war against Russia, so that Ukrainian blood is spilled for their own anti-Russian ideologies and geopolitical goals. This kind of warfare is downright vile. All peoples who suffered under the Soviet Union understandably bring with them scepticism towards the Russian Federation and, as we have read, this is absolutely justified by what they have experienced. However, these reservations should not stand in the way of a possible peace and international understanding. In view of the suffering civilian population, one should avoid linking one's personal vendetta desires against the Russians to this, especially if one is not directly affected. This conflict can only be resolved at the negotiating table and with compromises, and as quickly as possible. The longer the fighting drags on, the more young men and civilians die on both sides and the destruction continues. However, as long as the slogan is heard, even in USA Senate hearings, from politicians across Europe and in the media, that a Ukrainian victory over Russia is possible, even highly likely, and that arms deliveries continue to increase, the people of Ukraine are being given a false picture of the situation. Hopes are being raised and a willingness to make sacrifices is being created that have little in common with the real situation and the most likely outcome of this conflict. The destabilisation of the EU is also achieved with this unnecessary conflict. Attempts are being made to expand one's own spheres of influence in Eastern Europe, thereby creating new ones for current allies. New fault lines are also being created in Eastern Europe. The danger of an escalation of the conflict is accepted by the USA and almost longed for by Poland in order to realise its own far-reaching geopolitical goals, which include the lasting weakening of Russia.

What you should know about Ukraine.

In order to be able to assess facts correctly, one needs sufficient knowledge. Especially in such a difficult situation, in which Ukraine and ultimately all of Europe, including Russia, find themselves, it is particularly important to have the basics for a correct analysis. Therefore, here are some essential facts about Ukraine that tend to go unmentioned in the media coverage, especially since last year.

After the collapse of the Soviet Union, a referendum on independence was held in Ukraine (notwithstanding the administrative shambles the country was then in) on 1st December 1991. 90.3% of Ukrainians who actually voted are said to have voted in favour. In Crimea, on the other hand, only slightly more than half agreed to independence from Russia. Despite the rather clear desire for independence, it became apparent that the post-Soviet period was a very difficult one for Ukraine and its citizens. People were searching for a national identity and a clear definition of their own goals and international tasks; but the nation remained torn in many areas. This was very clear from the way people in the individual Ukrainian oblasts voted and which primary language was primarily spoken there. Especially in the east and southeast of Ukraine, the majority of the people are pure Russian speakers and also tend to feel more connected to Russia. In the absence of trust in the state leadership and the Ukrainians' urge to go to the glittering West, a strong emigration movement towards the West quickly began. 6.5 million people have already left Ukraine since 1991.

When talking about national identities in Ukraine and ethnic tensions, it is particularly important to take a little discourse into history, especially with regard to the current conflict. Kievan Rus, in any form, is the cradle of what became the Grand Duchy of Moscow and the subsequent Tsarist Empire. After the collapse of Kievan Rus due to the strong and incessant attacks of the Mongol hordes of horsemen from the East, there were large numbers of people from this region who migrated north-eastwards and thus entered the territory of the Moscow Grand Duchy and the Tsarist Empire, which they all helped to build. Kievan Rus was very similar in it's structure to the Holy Roman Empire of the German Nation. It was also a collection of principalities united under one ruler. Their habitat covered an area from present-day Moldavia to Lake Onega, high in the north. The rule of the Scandinavian-born ruler Ryurik began in Novgorod in 862ad.

He was the founder of the Rurikrid tribe and was chosen as the unifying ruler at the request of the quarrelling Slavic tribes. Originally referring only to the tribe, the term Rus later became a geographical definition of the territory of the Rus tribe. After the capture of what was then a small trading town, Kiev, in 882ad, the ruler moved from Novgorod to Kiev and the name of the empire, Kievan Rus, was established. Basically, it can be said that a large part of today's Russians and Ukrainians have a common political-cultural-religious origin and are people who lived together more or less peacefully for centuries. To try to differentiate between native Russians and Ukrainians is therefore demonstrably historical nonsense. For this reason, it is again brought home to us that it is mostly not peoples who start wars, but their princes, kings and presidents who are guided by power, interests and greed.

As we have seen, emigration was a major problem in Ukraine after its declared independence. Economically, Ukraine also went steadily downhill. In 2020, Ukraine's gross domestic product (GDP), adjusted for inflation, was only 69.3% of what it was in 1990. What is quite remarkable about this, is the fact that even the various financial injections from the EU and the USA failed to change this decline. By 2019, more than 20 billion euros in economic aid[48] had been disbursed to Ukraine. 15 billion from the EU alone.[49] Military support since February 2022 is tens of times higher again. The military and economic support totals well over one hundred billion euros, which have flowed to Ukraine from various pots.[50]

Capital flight, reform backlog, emigration and outdated technology are major factors for poor economic performance. The overshadowing problem in Ukraine, however, is the rampant corruption in the state. Bribery and nepotism are the agenda in Ukraine. Even in such tense and tragic times since February 2022, when Ukraine's sovereignty and self-determination are at stake, there is no let-up in the greed of the influential and powerful. Weapons from Western aid deliveries have already been discovered on the black market in Ukraine. Several ministers have already been removed from the government for corruption and bribery, but this all seems like a cosmetic correction, as even Ukrainian President Volodymyr Zelenskyi, since the "Panama and Pandora Papers"[51], does not have a clean slate. 41 million euros is a proud sum that has accumulated in his "offshore"[52] accounts[53]. Zelenskyi has also acquired a considerable real estate portfolio. Luxury houses in Kiev and even a villa in Tuscany, which he wanted to sell some time ago for 4.5 million euros and unfortu-

[48] https://www.wsws.org/de/articles/2019/11/23/ukra-n23.html

[49] https://ec.europa.eu/commission/presscorner/detail/en/MEMO_15_5035

[50] https://www.ifw-kiel.de/topics/war-against-ukraine/ukraine-support-tracker/?cookie-Level=not-set

[51] 49 https://www.theguardian.com/news/2021/oct/03/revealed-anti-oligarch-ukrainian-president-offshore-connections-volodymyr-zelenskiy

[52] 50 https://offshoreleaks.icij.org/search?c=UKR

[53] 51 https://www.occrp.org/en/the-pandora-papers/pandora-papers-reveal-offshore-holdings-of-ukrainian-president-and-his-inner-circle

nately forgot to declare it as property when he ran for office.[54] It is also astonishing who, among others, financially supported Zelenskyi's candidacy. On the one hand, he made points with his campaign to finally counter corruption decisively, but on the other hand he allowed himself to be massively supported by one of the richest oligarchs in the country, Ihor Kolmoisky, who is said to have amassed his fortune through corruption and fraud.[55]

As the saying goes, money doesn't stink and the behaviour of the Ukrainians seems to be pathological in a way. If you look at the behaviour of some of the Ukrainian "refugees", hundreds of thousands of whom are streaming into Germany and receiving full social benefits upon application, but who then get back on the bus or in their car to Kiev after submitting their application, you at least start to have doubts about the situation as well as the righteousness. Another observation the author made himself, showed that there are many young Ukrainian men who are not allowed to be in Germany because they are banned from leaving the country and required to fight the Russians. In the meantime, they can be found everywhere with their western modern cars. Here, too, it becomes clear that money in Ukraine can buy one's way out of the obligation to defend the fatherland with weapons. But desertion cannot be ruled out here either. The author cannot even blame these young men negatively, because under the given circumstances and with reference to an honest assessment of the situation, there is a good chance that they would have given their lives in a war in which it is not even clear that everything was really done, by both sides, to prevent it and the suffering of the civilian population. A final

[54] 52 https://www.occrp.org/en/daily/9479-popular-presidential-candidate-failed- to-declare-italian-villa

[55] 53 https://eurasianet.org/a-brief-history-of-corruption-in-ukraine-the-dawn-of-the-zelensky-era

grouping that has been encountered far more frequently in the major cities of Europe since the outbreak of the war is the Ukrainian elites. Those who can get away with anything in Ukraine with money, since just about everyone in Ukraine can be bribed. These people, driving their Bentleys, Ferraris, BMWs and Rolls Royces, on central and western European roads, seem to care very little about the course of the war and the fate of their compatriots, even though they have built their fortunes on the shoulders of these people, which, however, is now in safe accounts abroad.

The 2004 presidential elections were overshadowed by alleged electoral fraud, the attempted assassination of Viktor Yushchenko and the proven involvement of the Konrad-Adenauer Foundation and USA NGOs, including the Open Society Foundation (founded and directed by George Soros), whose goal is to bring "democracy" and a free society to the world and to bring to each country the kind of "democracy" that George Soros believes is right. The fact that his liberal and globalist ideas and the implementation of this ideology by intervening in the internal affairs of a country by financing protest groups violates basic democratic values may perhaps only be marginally significant. The interested reader may ask how these manipulative interventions take place. This can be explained relatively easily on the basis of the so-called colour revolutions. The author takes the liberty of quoting "Wikipedia" directly on this for good reason.

"Colour revolutions is a term for unarmed, mostly peaceful, but not always non-violent transformations since the early 2000s, which are named after an identification-forming colour or after a plant that is generally regarded as positive (such as tulip, cedar). Initiators and bearers of these revolutions were often students."

and another quote on the involvement of the USA:

"'The Washington Post' reported that the USA used $77 million in the run-up to the Yugoslav elections of 24 September 2000. Among other things, it was used to provide opposition parties with computers, fax machines and other office equipment and to train their members for party work. A New York firm had also collected opinion polls in Serbia. Trade unions and student groups also received money. The operation had been closely coordinated with European 'allies' and had been partly channelled through Hungary. Financial resources for the payment of trainers and campaign managers of the colour revolutions have so far flowed mainly from the USA and Western Europe. One of the best-known trainers was Robert Helvey, a former employee of the US military intelligence agency DIA. The USA foundations Freedom House and National Endowment for Democracy (NED) as well as George Soros' private foundation, Open Society Institute, provided several million US dollars. An article in the 'New York Times' in April 2011 confirmed the systematic training of youth by US institutions. Named was a 2008 meeting in New York City for Egyptian activists supported by Facebook, Google, Columbia Law School and the State Department."

In the list of sources at the end of the book, you will find further references on the topic. However, one thing is already clear. No demonstration organised by a few students without a clever marketing concept and sufficient capital will take on a scale that will ultimately be perceived beyond the borders. An example of how contrived and self-satisfied this foundation of George Soros acts is the announcement that it wants to get involved in Germany because it observes with concern the growing strength of the "Alternative for Germany" party, which in its view is developing too positively.

"We are looking at ways to support actors in eastern Germany who share our values," Selmin Caliskan, director at the Open Society Foundation, said in Berlin.[56] *"As a first step, we will be launching a local initiative to combat 'hate crimes' in and around eastern Berlin, together with local partners,"* Çaliskan announced. Details would be announced in the coming months.

According to Çaliskans, the foundation supports about 50 civil society organisations in Germany. In Kiev, as in Yugoslavia and Georgia, it was a youth and student organisation called "Pora!" that played a not insignificant role in the Orange Revolution in 2004. Here, too, there is evidence that proves the involvement of the foundations already mentioned. The Orange Revolution was supposed to clear the way for Ukraine towards the West, towards the EU. However, it turned out shortly afterwards that the two protagonists Viktor Yushchenko and Yulia Tymoshenko did not manage to agree on a common path for the good of Ukraine. The Orange camp had already fallen out shortly after the 2004 elections and Tymoshenko was dismissed as prime minister by Yushchenko.[57] This led to great disappointment among the population. The receipt came with the 2010 presidential elections, which were won by the pro-Russian Viktor Yanukovych. In the years that followed, attempts were of course made by the Russian side to tie Ukraine more firmly to Russia again. When the EU Association Agreement was not ratified by Yanukovych in November 2013, the first protests took place on the Maidan shortly afterwards, on 1 December. Despite further assurances from Russia and the Russian announcement to grant Ukraine a loan of 15 billion dollars, the protests did not stop. On

[56] https://www.welt.de/politik/deutschland/article195664047/Soros-Stiftung-erwaegt-wegen-der-AfD-Engagement-in-Deutschland.html

[57] https://www.welt.de/politik/ausland/article125126222/Wie-Janukowitsch-nur-huebscher-und-mit-Zopf.html

22nd January 2014, the first two people were killed. Less than a month later, there were serious riots with more than 60 deaths. Despite the efforts of the German and French foreign ministers and an agreement to prepare for new elections in May of the same year, the protesters could not be calmed down. Yanukovych fled Ukraine on 22nd February 2014, fearing for his life.

The tragedy on the Maidan - an important turning point?

It should be mentioned at the outset that the process of coming to terms with the events on the Maidan has not been completed to everyone's satisfaction up until this day. Relatively shortly after the bloody protests, the Ukrainian government delivered a short document, which, however, left many questions unanswered. It was apparently enough to state as a fact that the police officers of the "Berkut Беркут" ("Golden Eagles"), a special unit of the Ukrainian militia under the Ministry of Interior, were the first to fire on the demonstrators. The problem is that depending on who you talk to, you hear very different and contradictory statements. The investigation of the events has been relatively difficult from the beginning, as much evidence was destroyed immediately after the shootings[58]. Some witnesses claim that people were deliberately killed by snipers. An unnamed member of the Ukrainian parliament testified at the time that snipers fired from rooftops at police and demonstrators alike. In 2015, the theory of

---

[58] https://www.welt.de/politik/article137679769/Das-Maidan-Blutbad-bleibt-noch-immer-raetselhaft.html

snipers on rooftops was dismissed by Ukrainian investigators as untenable due to lack of evidence. In his reasoning, the investigator stated that most of the demonstrators were killed by shots fired from Kalashnikovs. The question of the others killed remains, for the time being. According to him, the policemen were killed with hunting rifles and pistols. Another witness stated that on 20th of February he had been on duty as a Red Cross volunteer behind the police barricades and had seen two policemen killed there, who according to him had been shot with a hunting rifle. These statements raise several questions: On the one hand, why someone would draw attention to hunting rifles several times in a newspaper article and in the same breath want to weaken the statements and assumptions about sniper rifles. On the other hand, it remains to be clarified how different hunting rifles and sniper rifles actually are and, above all, whether they could be easily distinguished from a distance by laypersons who made observations as eyewitnesses. Externally, there are only minor differences between these two types of rifles. Both are mostly bolt action rifles and are equipped with a telescopic sight. If only the calibre could be checked. Here, too, the similarities are very clear. Mostly the calibre .308 is used, or in Russian models 7.62 x 39 R Mosin-Nagant. There are a few other calibres, but they are less common. Furthermore, it is necessary to find out to what extent one could distinguish a difference in the entry wounds as a non-trained forensic pathologist, in the case of two similar or identical projectiles from different weapons. The answer is: it is not possible. Corresponding statements are thus not only useless, but presumably all come from the realm of fantasy of the persons who are trying to obstruct the clarification of this tragedy. On 10th of April 2014, the WDR (West Deutscher Rundfunk) television magazine "Monitor" reported, that shots were fired at demonstrators at least not only by the snipers deployed by

Yanukovych, but also by other snipers who possibly belonged to the camp of the opposition at the time.[59]

It seems reasonable to assume that the one-sided, obfuscating articles, which abounded in the German-language and Western press, were intended to distract the reader from the possibility that there were snipers who may have fired at police officers and demonstrators alike, which would have very convincingly supported the theory of a targeted escalation. Despite the apparent attempt to conceal the details, many in Ukraine are now convinced that there was a third force that calculatedly caused an escalation on the Maidan, including Andrij Parubi, who was deputy speaker of the Ukrainian parliament from 2015 and commander of the Maidan Self-Defence in 2014. He claims there were no weapons on the protesters' side. He was on the Maidan on the morning of 20th of February and reported, that the first deaths occurred on the side of the demonstrators at around 8:00 o'clock. At the same time, he said, he had received a text message from MP Andriy Shevchenko, who was himself in contact with a "Berkut" commander. Shevchenko wrote to him, that the policemen were being shot at with live ammunition1. This allegedly happened from the conservatory, which was under the control of the demonstrators at the time. Andrij Parubi reported that he had sent his men to search the building but found no shooters. However, there are photos taken that morning at the conservatory by a Ukrainian photographer showing people with "hunting rifles". The BBC had apparently been able to speak to one of the protesters shooting from the conservatory at the time.[60] He said he had not meant to kill anyone, but had merely shot at the feet of the police officers. And

[59] https://www1.wdr.de/daserste/monitor/videos/video-todesschuesse-in-kiew-wer-ist-fuer-das-blutbad-vom-maidan-verantwortlich-100.html

[60] https://theworld.org/stories/2015-02-12/sniper-tells-bbc-he-may-have helped-provoke-massacre-ukraine

again, reference is made here to a hunting rifle and further the statements remain contradictory:[61]

According to the BBC report, after the first exchange of fire, the police retreated. The Maidan demonstrators followed the police. The police then fired from submachine guns at all the demonstrators who ran towards them. The next lines contain the original wording of the Ukrainian investigator Donskoj. "None of the demonstrators who were injured and killed on 20th of February were carrying weapons". At the same time, no one was killed or arrested by those who shot at police officers. For this reason, the prosecution does not assume in the case of the "Berkut" policemen that they acted in self-defence. After the author had viewed various videos showing the events on the Maidan, it is obvious that the portrayal of unarmed demonstrators is not tenable. The firing of pistols is clearly visible, as is the use of "hunting rifle" with a sighting device and Moletov cocktails thrown at police officers. Police officers lying on the ground and still being attacked by demonstrators show that the violence was not one-sided. There is absolutely no question of innocent and defenceless demonstrators being attacked, as the available videos and pictures clearly prove. It is also clear that the demonstrators are acting systematically. There are coordinators who tell them exactly where barricades are to be set up and where people are to position themselves. The statements on the tragedy are very opaque, illogical and sometimes sound extremely contrived, but it is becoming increasingly clear that there was a third force on the Maidan that caused the escalation by shooting at police officers and demonstrators alike. The question remains: who or what was this third force? If you talk to Ukrainians, Poles or Balts, it was clearly the Russians. In March 2014, the Ukrainian Interior Minister Arsen Avakov named this "third force" as

---

[61] https://www.youtube.com/watch?v=mJhJ6hks0Jg

something like the USSR will arise again. abc

Protestor on the Maidan: Equipped with helmet, protective shield, gas mask and baton.

A protestor fires at police officers with a hunting rifle.

The "coordinator" directing the protestors to their positions.

Policemen protect themselves from the protester's attack.

"non-Ukrainian". He expressed the opinion that Russia was behind the snipers. President Poroshenko expressed the same opinion a year after the events. The further one gets towards the West, however, the more people suspect that the West is behind this apparently deliberate escalation. A not insignificant number of average citizens - i.e. none of the so-called experts, leading media journalists or politicians of the leading parties - consider it very likely that these protests and the resulting possibility of a change of political direction were prepared and fuelled by the USA. After all, there are already indications of something similar in connection with the "Arab Spring" in various North African states, which resulted, among other things, in the aforementioned cruel assassination of Libyan leader Ghaddafi.

We have already been able to clearly demonstrate the influence of American think tanks on the Orange Revolution. In this case, there is nothing actually watertight or any generally available evidence that unquestionably links one side or the other to the deeds on the Maidan. Knowing the details of what actually happened on the days in question in February 2014 would be extremely helpful in order to be able to better assess the subsequent events up to the present day. One thing is clear, however: this was not a spontaneous reaction from the population to a rejection of the EU Association Agreement. It was far too well organised for that and it was never intended to be just a peaceful demonstration, as evidenced in particular by the protective gear with which most of the protesters had equipped themselves in advance. The huge quantities of car tyres also had to be brought in, as well as many other materials for building barricades.

This major geopolitical event had an enormous impact on political developments in the Ukraine, its relationship with Russia and Russia's relationship with NATO and the EU. It may even have been the event that sparked the disastrous developments that followed in the Ukraine. Who could have benefited more from these events and the subsequent overthrow with the ousting of the pro-Russia President Yanukovych: Russia or the USA? Let us try to analyse the matter as neutrally as possible and come up with two hypotheses:

Hypothesis one:

Russia did it! Russia moved snipers into position for the purpose of escalating an already highly tense situation. Yanukovych ordered the "Berkut" units to act aggressively against the demonstrators. What fundamental goal would the Russian side have wanted to pursue with this? Was it possibly an attempt to restore order through chaos and fear? Was it an attempt to divert attention from a possibly already planned annexation of Crimea, or to create a solid reason for it? In the context of what we know and in view of the fact that a pro-Russian government was in power in Kiev, which gradually promoted an amicable relationship between the two states with the Russian leadership, this hypothesis does not seem convincing. Admittedly, V. Yanukovych was not a particularly popular president, as he too was addicted to money and power in an inappropriate and illegal manner. Nepotism and corruption were also the order of the day in this Ukrainian government and a typical feature of the young Ukrainian state from the very beginning. We should further take into account that as late as 17th of December, Russian President Putin made an attempt to ease the situation by holding out the prospect of a $15 billion loan to the Ukraine and assuring favourable gas prices. In return, Russia demanded accession to the Eurasian Economic Union. The question remains, however, which course of action would have been most beneficial to Russia's goals. Strategically, Russia could only lose with an escalation of this kind. And risking the resignation or fall of the pro-Russian President Yanukovych would certainly have been anything but a clever move in the present situation. President Yanukovych's suspension of the Association Agreement with the EU is seen as the start of the Maidan protests. A tough approach might have been understandable if the majority of Ukrainians had actually been in favour of turning to the West and joining the EU, and if there had been a fear of the population drifting towards the EU. But that was not the case. The Research Centre for Eastern Europe in Bremen found in its studies that in the years 2004 to 2014 the acceptance of EU membership was only 30 to a maximum of 40 percent. A referendum would have been enough to finally clarify the situation. Interestingly, the number of supporters of a renewed rapprochement with Russia was at a similar level.[62] After the events on the Maidan, the picture changed abruptly in the direction of the EU. Now 52.3 per cent of the population were in favour of joining the EU. This was despite the fact that, according to statistics, only 18 percent of Ukrainians even knew what was written in the agreement.

Hypothesis two:

The USA did it! What would have been the advantages and disadvantages of intervention on their part? It has never been a secret that the USA and NATO have defined the integration of Ukraine into the West as a strategic goal for quite some time. At the latest since the NATO summit in Bucharest in 2008, this was publicly declared a primary USA/NATO goal.

---

[62] https://www.laender-analysen.de/ukraine/pdf/UkraineAnalysen127.pdf Artikel: Zwischen Chaos und autoritärer Machtsicherung S.18

This goal is of central importance from an economic and strategic point of view and has been stringently adhered to ever since, since Ukraine's wealth of resources, apart from Russia, is unique in Europe and Ukraine also occupies a strategically and geographically important position. It is not for nothing, for example, that Ukraine has long been considered the breadbasket of Europe. Strategically, it is extremely important for NATO and the USA to be able to place their allies and bases directly on Russia's doorstep and at the same time to detach Ukraine from Russia's sphere of influence. Thus, the two great powers have opposing objectives with regard to Ukraine, which, given everything we have already read, must inevitably lead to a confrontation. Ukraine is historically, culturally and politically the cradle of Russia and an important part of Russian identity and nationhood until the dissolution of the Soviet Union. Since the dissolution of the Soviet Union and until a few years ago, an important neighbour and trading partner of the Russian Federation. Furthermore, with the naval Black Sea port of Sevastopol, of central importance for Russia in terms of military strategy. It is obvious that Russia would by no means accept the USA and NATO gaining a foothold in Ukraine and, in addition, being completely excluded economically and politically via EU membership. In this context, it seems inevitable that the actions of the Western powers, first and foremost the USA, has led to tensions here. From a geostrategic point of view, the USA's goal would be to do everything possible to steer the Ukraine into the "safe haven of the West". The measures that would be necessary for this would have to be sustainable and irreversible, so that a renewed overturning by a pro-Russian government would never again be possible.

Giving the impression that the Yanukovych government, which is allied with the Russian government, had demonstrators deliberately shot or that the Russians themselves were partly responsible for the escalation on the Maidan would achieve the greatest possible effect. The reputation of the Russians would thus have reached an all-time low. As we know, it would not be the first time that demonstrators in Ukraine were led by American NGOs in advance to ignite the desired momentum. The opinion of Ukrainians about EU accession before the events on the Maidan also suggests that it was strategically imperative for the West, or rather the US, to take appropriate measures to bring about an adjustment of public opinion towards pro-Western in the Ukraine. Nevertheless, for most people, regardless of which country they live in and from which perspective they perceive this, it remains a question of faith who fired first and thus caused the escalations. A decision made on the basis of gut instinct and personal dislike of one side or the other is not particularly helpful and clouds the view of the essentials.

With the greatest respect for the victims, however, it is an absolute duty to be neutral in the analysis and always committed to the truth and it's discovery. There is currently no conclusive evidence in the available media to link one side or the other to the crime without any doubt. The events described allow only one conclusion: to cast doubt in all clarity on the official version disseminated in our leading media, according to which the security organs of the then Ukrainian Yanukovych government fired shots at unarmed and peaceful opposition demonstrators. Even in the case of the Russians, the hardest evidence is at best scraps of intercepted phone calls that have not been presented in full to the public. Without access to all the facts, an assessment is always a game of vabanque. The author reserves the right to make his own personal assessment in an attempt to maintain the necessary neutrality. In any case, further facts will be gathered in order to hopefully gain the necessary insights at a later date that may lead to a final assessment of what really happened. Should you as a reader have further information or know of safe, reputable sources, the author would be pleased to hear from you. At this point, an urgent appeal can be made to the readers not to prematurely believe the circulating rumours, descriptions and propaganda, as the search for the truth can quickly end in a maze of assumptions and bias due to personal dislikes. Unfortunately, it is also a fact that the leading media in various countries, especially in Germany and Britain, are part of the propaganda battle and do not provide objective help in finding the truth. As mentioned, a large part of the evidence was destroyed immediately after the incident. The investigations are obviously progressing deliberately, exceedingly slowly, and to this day there is no official final result of the investigation into the tragic incidents on the Maidan. In the following, an example circulating on the internet, which at first glance seems absolutely plausible, will show how confusion is to be created with false representations and constructed stories:

Reports are circulating of an Italian video production claiming that three Georgian snipers fired the shots on the Maidan on the orders of former President Zakashvili (2004 to 2013). It also mentioned the involvement of a former USA military officer who allegedly gave detailed instructions to the snipers. However, according to research, this account does not stand up to scrutiny. On the one hand, Sakashvili was no longer president at the time, and on the other hand, one of the alleged snipers was still in Georgian custody at the time. The security passes shown in the documentary have spelling mistakes and different spellings and make a very unprofessional impression. The alleged Georgian mastermind Mamuka Mamulashvili, who is supposed to have set everything up, has denied these accounts in writing as untrue. The fact that he is a self-confessed Russia-hater, on the other hand, would fit the picture. Another thing seems somewhat disreputable in this context. Sakashvilli was suddenly made a presidential advisor to Viktor Poroshenko, who was elected in May 2014. Nevertheless, all this does not change the fact that this story cannot be backed up with solid evidence, but contains various contradictions. This is a good example of how quickly false or, at best, half-true accounts can start to unintentionally draw false conclusions, which can subsequently lead to even more irritation and controversy. They play right into the hands of those who exploit these controversies to further obscure the actual facts.

All that we have read on the subject of the Maidan and the events in Ukraine at that time represents only a small part of what should actually be reported on for the sake of good order. Due to the topicality of the book, the author refrains from further elaboration in this first edition. However, it is a matter of decency not to leave an important scene of this time completely unmentioned, since 48 people met a horrible death there. We are speaking about Odessa on May 2nd 2014. Here, a deadly hunt was organised for pro-Russian anti-Maidan demonstrators, which ended with the 48 people seeking shelter in the local trade union building being burnt alive in agony. A pro-Ukrainian mob, interspersed with violent neo-Nazis, did not let the people escape from the burning building. Anyone who tried was murdered outside the building or died trying to jump out of the burning building. The alarmed fire brigade did not arrive until 40 minutes after the emergency call and the police, who were already on the scene, did not intervene despite the brutal attacks. Here, too, the investigation was massively obstructed by the Ukrainian authorities, so obviously that in 2016 the Office of the United Nations High Commissioner for Human Rights spoke out and sharply criticised this procedure. Further details and background information will follow in the 2nd edition of this book.

A Tense Relationship:
Russia and her neighbours.

For the most part, the Soviet Union was nothing more than a spectre for people in the West, which, according to politicians and the media, wanted to spread to Western Europe like an octopus. NATO was there to ensure that this did not happen. So much for the West's perfect world of deterrence and defence. None of this had any effect on everyday life in the West. It was characterised by an economic upswing and relatively great individual freedom. In Eastern Europe, things looked somewhat different, and a look at the history of the past century clearly shows us that before the Soviet Union, territorial claims against Russia's immediate neighbours already existed in the times of the Tsarist Empire and many territories were annexed. With the communist October Revolution and the emergence of the Soviet Union, expansionist aspirations reached their sad climax. Life in the Soviet Union and especially in the annexed republics, which were still quasi-independent states in the early 20th century, was far more difficult, determined by constraints and hardship, and all too often proved to be a challenge.

The imperialist thoughts of the Soviet rulers rarely knew any bounds in their contempt for their smaller neighbours. Anyone who was not already a proper communist was considered an enemy of the Communist Revolution, bourgeois or otherwise a subversive and disruptive element. Other political systems, cultures, language, or religion were not tolerated. Suppression, deportation, and even the murder and forced labour of hundreds of thousands of people in Soviet gulags are not horror stories born of a fertile imagination, but were the brutal reality that not only countless Russians themselves, but also the neighbouring countries of the Soviet Union were exposed to for decades after Red October 1917. In addition, neighbouring countries such as Poland and the Baltic States were already occupied by Russia, and Finland was a Grand Duchy but in Russia all the same, during the Tsarist era. In the Russo-Swedish War of 1808-1809, Russia had conquered Finland from Sweden. Only in the summer of 1919, and after a civil war lasting more than a year, did Finland become an independent state with the proclamation of a Republic. In the Second World War, Finland resisted an attack by the Soviet Union in a heroic winter defensive struggle in 1939-1940, but nevertheless temporarily lost parts of Finland's territory. In the hope of recovering that territory, Finland then supported Germany in the war against the Soviet Union.[63]

The fear of "the Russians" does not come from nowhere. Aversion and special caution results from the past experiences of the Balts, Finns, Poles, and, since 1992, Belarusians, Ukrainians and others, and this should be known, respected and kept in mind when making one-sided pro-Russian statements. After the fall of the Iron Curtain, the disintegration of the Soviet Union in 1991, and the dissolution of the Warsaw Pact from then onwards, the Russian leadership missed the historic opportunity to improve relations with its neighbours and to initiate an era of peaceful co-existence through understanding and co-operation, thus simultaneously striving for a relaxation of tensions in Eastern Europe. No words of apology, no gestures of reparation or anything similar passed the lips of the Russian leadership. On the contrary, the Soviet period was glorified again, as already mentioned, and the victims of the communist system were mocked in an intolerable manner. If Russia wants to be a respected member of the European community of states, it must accept responsibility for

---

[63] https://en.wikipedia.org/wiki/History_of_Finland

the mistakes that have been made and make it clear that Russia, or rather the Russian Federation, will in future strive for a partnership-based relationship with its Eastern European neighbours. This would not only be a sign of goodwill to finally put away the bloody waistcoat of the Soviet Union, it would be a new beginning capable of raising international understanding in Europe to a new level. In the same breath, however, it would also be good for a few other states in Europe to come to terms with their own historical actions instead of constantly demanding this of Germany alone in a prayer-like repetition. The assertion of Germany's sole responsibility for the beginning of the world wars does not stand up to historical scrutiny; this should be clear, in spite of all the efforts otherwise made. The author himself did not get to know Russia and the Russians as many of his Eastern European friends did during the Soviet era. This can certainly be an advantage, as it enables one to view the current situation from a neutral point of view. In his own trips to Eastern Europe and in conversations about Russia, the author was able to learn a lot about how people from the former Soviet republics dealt with their situation, how they lived while trying to preserve their own culture. So it was possible to learn how to approach Russia and what caution to exercise.

Later, after the period of the official Allied "Soviet Occupied Zone" (SBZ) and the subsequent founding of the German Democratic Republic in 1949, the Soviet Union was somewhat more cautious in its dealings with the GDR. People were allowed their own culture, their own characteristics and a certain independence, even in foreign policy. Despite the horrors of the war, the Soviets were possibly still aware that it was very beneficial for both nations if they and Germany maintained a good relationship with each other. Even though it was only a small part of Germany and the possibilities were limited, German engineers and workers in the

GDR always demonstrated their skills, which in many cases benefited the Soviet Union. Germany and Russia complement each other particularly well in economic terms, through research, technology, industrial development and structure on the one hand and an almost inexhaustible wealth of resources and industriousness on the other. Therefore, a friendly relationship between the two nations is desirable. At the same time, however, this is and has always been feared by other states, above all the USA and Poland. If you look at social media and the generally prevailing views in Germany, you notice relatively quickly that there are few people who take a neutral stance towards the great powers. One finds either USA/NATO supporters or a hearty "Russia understander". The author finds it necessary to reproduce some comments of the latter group of people:

"Putin free us once again."

"When the Russians come, I'll raise the Russian flag."

"Let the Russians invade, then at least our government will be deposed and there won't be any more gender-bending."

Such forgetfulness of history is remarkable. In the meantime, there are no fundamental differences in this attitude between West Germans and former GDR citizens; however, regional differences in sympathy for Russia tend to be recognisable in the federal states, i.e. the area of the former GDR. The vast majority of West Germans understand the representations and actions of the USA or "the West", which means mainly the NATO countries as a collective. Many seem to have forgotten that the invasion of Germany by the Red Army in 1945 was anything but a liberation. Numerous records as well as conversations with contemporary witnesses clearly show that rape, mistreatment of civilians and arbitrary murder or deportation occurred en masse in the Soviet-occupied zone after the Second World War and caused years of fear and trauma. The author's grandparents also knew such things. These facts must not be forgotten or suppressed. In the GDR, too, there was paternalism and attacks on civilians by the Soviets, and reparations were also demanded. A justifiable distrust of the declarations and intentions of the plutocratic USA and actors closely linked to its interests should not lead to a one-sided glorification of the other side, i.e. Russia.

And no, before there is any misunderstanding, the Western Allies acted just as ruthlessly and inhumanely during the war as they did after the surrender of Germany, on 8th of May 1945, and disregarded war Conventions.[64] Even if the Allied belligerents could claim the validity of the all-participation clause[65] for themselves, they are at least morally guilty of a considerable degree. The large-scale bombardments of cities – a total of about 1,000 German cities were attacked from the air and often largely destroyed – were targeted attacks and terror against the civilian population and thus war crimes, but certainly not war-decisive, militarily necessary measures. The bombing of Dresden, shortly before the end of the war, which was known as a Red Cross city and had no air defences and was filled with large numbers of refugees from Silesia and other parts of East Germany, is often used as a synonym for this senseless cruelty, but it was only one of many cities that suffered comparable fate. Allied bombers also bombed workers' quarters near industrial plants, killing countless forced

---

[64] Hague Land Warfare Convention and Geneva Conventions

[65] It states that in the event of war, these conventions shall only apply if all states involved in the conflict are parties to the respective agreement. The participation of a country that has not acceded to the convention in question before the start of the conflict invalidates the validity of the convention for all other states involved.

labourers who were sometimes prisoners of war, which to this day seems to be taken for granted as collateral damage. Even after the surrender of the Wehrmacht, there was shelling of civilians from fighter planes, especially in the countryside, as contemporary witnesses have reported. The inhumane cramming of German soldiers under catastrophic hygienic conditions in the so-called Rhine meadow camps has been largely forgotten and suppressed today. They were denied proper prisoner-of-war status; they were exposed outdoors to the weather for months, usually without protection; thousands died of thirst, starvation, and disease. Germans were outlawed and deprived of rights in their destroyed and occupied country in all occupation zones. Kangaroo Courts were the order of the day. It is a phenomenon that seems to be very pronounced in Germany. People prefer to take sides with others, to collectively close their eyes instead of recognising the external enemy and identifying with their own side and the fate of Germany, recognising and defending their own interests. It is no exaggeration to say that the sting of mistrust towards the Russians runs deep among the Eastern European peoples, and this is essentially due to Russia's behaviour over the last century or so, especially during the time of the Soviet Union. But it is also in their hands to break down the mistrust and, through honest reappraisal and communication at eye level, to initiate a new era of Russian relations with its neighbours as an integral part of a new security and economic structure in Europe. Or should we say, in the meantime, it would have been in Russian hands. Let us hope that the child has not yet fallen into the well.

Poland's new role

Poland has recently been upgraded as the most important ally of the USA on the European continent, replacing Germany in this questionable role. There are certainly some reasons for this. On the one hand, it is certainly strategically more favourable in the current situation, in Central-Eastern Europe and thus closer to the current geopolitical hotspot. On the other hand, the Americans' simple realisation that since the Poles gained their freedom from the Soviet Union they are far easier to control in their own sense than has been the case in Germany over the past decades and is still the case today may also be significant; for even in the days of the Bonn Republic, i.e. until 1990/1, there was often great resistance to the wars as well as the armament and weapons stationing of the USA. Poland hates Russia; this needs no further diplomatically correct paraphrasing and is true, with only a few minor exceptions among the Polish population. This, in turn, plays perfectly into the hands of the USA, as it requires no persuasion whatsoever to pursue an unequivocally anti-Russian foreign policy, to impose sanctions, to supply weapons and, as we shall see, also to irresponsibly pursue provocative geopolitics that create predetermined breaking points in Eastern Europe. The USA is making excellent use of the old Polish desire for power and influence in Eastern Europe. The first step the USA took in implementing its geostrategy was to give Poland a sense of security and significance. The missile defence system, which we already talked about in detail in the NATO chapter, and the stationing of USA troops, currently a little more than 10,000 soldiers, in Poland, was enough for the comfortable feeling of security. The significance came with the nodding off of some projects in which Poland could re-declare its claim to leadership in Eastern Europe and old great power fantasies were revived, and Polish nationalism was of use to the USA/NATO. Again, the USA was quickly able to trick Poland into believing that it was a significant country and an important partner for them. We recall what the Polish-born compatriot Zbigniew Brzezinski had to say about partners of the USA in Europe, in the chapter "who conducts geopolitics in Europe?"

The Poles are now apparently convinced that in this constellation they are safe from the possible wrath of the Russians when they find out what other plans Warsaw is carrying around in its luggage. But perhaps the Russians are already aware of the deeper meaning behind the decisions made in Warsaw. With all the geographical and economic factors that play a role in geopolitics today, strategic planning also depends on knowledge of the mentalities, sensitivities, and ambitions of nations and governments. Knowing these can be of particular importance for the implementation of certain geostrategic goals. History in itself, but also the recent activities of the Polish government and politicians, have made it abundantly clear how stereotypical and undifferentiated Poland still is, both socially and politically. There is dogmatic adherence to enemy images, behavioural patterns and a world view that can only be described as limited. Examples include a one-sided perception of one's own country in a permanent victim role, an exaggerated national consciousness – or national chauvinism, which goes hand in hand with a conspicuous overestimation of themselves. What the Poles obviously do not understand very well is the fact that the USA has highly trained analysts, psychologists and strategists. They have understood just as little as most EU states that the USA has no partners but at best stooges, and also does nothing without ultimately gaining advantages, of whatever kind, for itself and that others will be the losers, regardless of whether this turns out to be to the detriment of the supposed partner in retrospect or whether the latter even becomes an enemy later on. History repeatedly demonstrates this way of dealing with others by the USA.

Equipped with such a psychological profile as that of the Poles, it is easy for the USA to play with the Poles, like Paganini on his Stradivarius.

At the moment, Poland has the backing of the USA and Great Britain for its ambitious efforts. Let us have a brief look at the activities of the Poles. Even before the outbreak of the Ukraine war in February 2022, Poland was expanding its influence in the region, virtually unnoticed by Western interests. Poland's efforts to bring Ukraine onto NATO's course was an important task, which was also jointly carried out with the USA. In the overall geopolitical view, Ukraine is now a significant counterweight for the USA/NATO to Russian influence in Eastern Europe. What is essential here is that the country must be kept free of Russian influences in the process. The aspiration to integrate Ukraine into NATO and the EU is the natural consequence of the current situation. However, it is only possible for Poland to increase its own influence in the region if it enters into a close relationship with Ukraine (part of which they had once occupied). For the Poles, therefore, it is much more a necessary alliance of convenience than one based on current understanding and historical friendship.[66] In the same way, in Poland's neighbouring states they have been working intensively to strengthen and influence Polish minorities and to extend their political influence in these countries into government circles.[67] Virtually unnoticed by the Western media, Poland has been pursuing its ambitions to create a new sphere of influence in Eastern Europe. They are thus

---

[66] Vgl. Lang, Kai-Olaf: Poland and the East. Poland's relations with Russia, Belarus and Ukraine in the context of European Eastern Policy. SWP-Comments, Juni 2005; Ochmann, Cornelius: Östliche Partnerschaft contra EU-Partnerschaftsabkommen mit Russland? Die Bedeutung des polnisch-russischen Verhältnisses für die Zukunft Europas. In: Polen-Analysen, Nr. 46/2009.

[67] https://www.lrt.lt/en/news-in-english/19/1400592/vilnius-cannot-exist-without-strong-polish-community-disputes-arise-in-every-home-pm

currently the only country in Europe, apart from the USA, that is actively pursuing geopolitics.

Let's have a brief look at the projects. First, there is the "Three Seas Initiative", inspired by a study by the USA's think tank "The Atlantic Council", which was launched in 2014 by Poland and, remarkably, Croatia. The structure currently comprises 12 countries. The deeper meaning of this connection is to make better use of the economic potential of the individual countries, to create new markets and structures in Eastern Europe. Of course, all this is to take place under Polish leadership. Above all, Poland wants to intensify its own influence on the Eastern European market. It is well known that Poland does not shy away from confrontations with the EU, so it is relatively easy to come up with a hypothesis that does not seem too strange. The creation of a zone of influence in Eastern Europe comparable to that of the European Union will lead to Poland, the country with the largest gross domestic product (GDP) in comparison to other Eastern European countries, wanting to take on a clear pioneering role also in economic terms and additionally creating a certain political dominance. Poland would thus set the tone economically in Eastern Europe. For this to happen, however, Russia must in any case be weakened more clearly and, if Polish ideas have their way, even broken up as a country. The withdrawal of several Eastern European states from the European Union would be conceivable in this case. The question would remain open as to what would be more important for these states, financial alienation by the EU or a turning away from the totalitarian paternalism policy of the European Union, which is also taking on worrying forms from a German point of view. In any case, the damage to the EU would be immense. Less so financially, since the donor countries and especially Germany would still be at the ready, but the economic damage, the reduction of the economic and political sphere of influence and the damaged reputation of the EU would be considerable. In general, it could raise the question of the raison d'être of this kind of EU. We don't even want to talk about the billions of euros already given by the donor countries. Another Polish project, however, has a very clear geopolitical character. This is already revealed by the name and the original idea behind the whole thing. It is the idea of the "Intermarium". The idea of the Intermarium originally came from Józef Klemens Piłsudski, the Polish dictator. In the early 1930s, he developed it in order to pursue two main goals. On the one hand, the Poles were trying to revive the Polish-Lithuanian Union, and on the other hand, they wanted to establish a structure that could have withstood both the Soviet Union and the German Reich. That Poland already had little or no political tact at the time became clear at the latest at the point where countries like Lithuania were expected to voluntarily submit to this Union and thus to return to Polish overlordship after over 200 years. On the one hand, Lithuania and other states had only recently regained their independence, and on the other hand, the Lithuanians and other peoples were still acutely aware of how badly they had been treated by the Poles in the past.[68] To believe that someone would voluntarily join this idea

STOSUNKI POLSKO - LITEWSKIE.

Marszałek Piłsudski. Naści, piesku, kiełbasę...
Piesek. Chochyście mi nawet Wilno dali, to zacznę szczekać o Grodno i Białystok, bo już taki jestem...

Poland is making fun of Lithuania's justified demands for the return of its capital.

---

[68] The part of Lithuania that came under Polish rule after 1920 clearly experienced repression in the form of the closure of schools and the persecution of Lithuanian political and cultural elites.

124

when they had more to lose than to gain in the process, especially their newly won independence, testifies to a far-reaching detachment from reality. The project failed miserably precisely because of the facts described above. Not one of the countries envisaged by Poland wanted to be voluntarily ruled or administered by Poland. The Intermarium, however, as mentioned, was intended to fulfill a second purpose, namely to demarcate Germany and Russia from each other politically and economically. One can conclude that the establishment of such a structure would have created enormous problems for the German as well as the Russian economy, which could have relatively quickly led to greater geopolitical tensions and ultimately to the outbreak of a major war as well. The latest current idea of the Intermarium with the planned/proposed participation of Latvia, Lithuania, Slovakia and Ukraine, again under Polish leadership of course, has exactly the same geopolitical goal. They believe they can pursue modern geopolitics getting their idea out of mothballs and hope that the current situation in Eastern Europe will help them to polish up their own image in order to make it easier to convince the other countries to join a union led by Poland. They even seem to be so convinced of themselves and the idea that they already include Belarus in it. Or is it, that they already know more about which country is to be destabilised next?[69] The fact that the general economic advantages primarily cited are intended to serve the Polish advantage can also be seen in the selected other players, whose combined GDP is just about equal to that of Poland. Thus, even in the case of the Intermarium, the Polish economy would be in a much better position to establish new sales markets in the smaller countries than vice versa. Tying the smaller markets to Poland, however it is done, would be equally

[69] https://rmx.news/poland/polish-general-poland-should-assist-any-uprising-in-belarus-and-overthrow-lukashenko-regime/?utm_source=newsletter&utm_medium=email&utm_cam-paign=ukraine_will_have_to_wait_for_now_for_nato_membership_germany_officially_enters_recession_and_a_polish_general_said_what&utm_term=2023-05-25

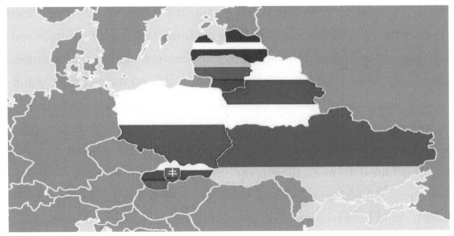

The Intermarium - Poland's dream of a leading role in Eastern Europe.

advantageous and cannot be ruled out, as it could at the same time damage the German economy, since the smaller countries currently obtain most of their goods from Germany. All this is currently happening not only under the eyes of the USA, but also with its consent. "Laissez faire" is the motto, as long as it fits into the geopolitical grid of the USA. Many of the activities currently being pursued by Poland play geopolitically into the hands of the USA, and it is only for this reason that things are being allowed to happen. Shortly after the start of the Ukraine war, Poland hastily tried to hand over MiG-29 fighter jets to Ukraine.[70]

A so-called ring swap was to take place, in which Poland was to receive modern F-16 jets from the USA as compensation. All this was to take place in Ramstein, an American air base in the Rhineland. Let us briefly summarise: A NATO member wants to hand over fighter jets to a non-member state, which is currently at war with Russia. All this was to take place on the territory of another NATO member. A third NATO member

---

[70] https://www.diepresse.com/6109224/polen-will-alle-seine-mig-29-jets-den-usa-zur-verfuegung-stellen

holds weapons on the territory of the second NATO member, which the first NATO member receives as compensation. As icing on the cake, the MiGs should then be flown directly from Ramstein to Ukraine. Just reading this can make one dizzy, but the idea of wanting to implement something like this while insisting on not becoming a party to the war itself is hard to imagine. Fortunately, this action was called off because it caused controversy even in the Western media and at that point the USA was unwilling to continue with it if the media interest was too strong. The impact of an alleged Russian missile behind Poland's eastern border was also quickly sensationalised by the Poles, who hoped to use it for their own propaganda campaign against Russia. Unfortunately, it soon turned out to be a missile launched by Ukraine itself. The most recent example of Polish provocation was directly directed against an ally, namely Germany. Poland announced in mid-January 2023 that it was handing over German-built and licensed Leopard 2 tanks to Ukraine. A good week after the anouncement, after there had apparently not yet been any approval from the German government, Poland's representatives stood in front of the press and announced audibly for the whole world that they would nevertheless deliver the tanks to Ukraine if Germany did not give its approval.[71] The announcement of a breach of contract on a bilateral level in front of the world press had never been made in this form before. The pressure built up by the USA, Poland, Ukraine, and even Lithuania in the media borders on disrespect for state sovereignty and democratic decision-making. The decision to supply heavy battle tanks was subsequently taken in a cabinet meeting of the German government and not decided by a public vote in the German parliament. The fact that Poland has committed more than a diplomatic faux pas here does not really seem to interest anyone in the

---

[71] https://www.theguardian.com/world/2023/jan/23/poland-ready-to-send-tanks-to-ukraine-without-german-consent

international public arena. The announcement of a deliberate violation of a treaty between two states in the case of heavy weapons of war can hardly be surpassed in audacity. The fact that this is obviously a political line currently being pursued by the Poles is shown by the fact that they are not keeping to agreements made, even economically. As recently as December 2022, Germany and Poland agreed to supply the PCK refinery in Schwedt with oil, among other things, as soon as Germany stopped purchasing Russian crude oil via the Druzhba pipeline. Now the Polish side is refusing to implement the deliveries on the grounds that the ownership situation has not been explained to it in a sufficiently conclusive manner.[72] It is not sufficient that the German trust company has taken over the shares of the Russian Rosneft group until further notice because of the sanctions imposed. Poland itself, however, still buys oil from Russia and intends to purchase around 3 million tonnes in 2023. Economists are convinced that this was an economic policy move in order to be able to buy up the refinery, which may now be in economic difficulties, cheaply, through its own oil company Orlen. A similar manoeuvre has already been concluded in Lithuania. Whatever the motivation behind it, it is another breach of an agreement reached between Germany and Poland.

One point that underlines Poland's provocative behaviour like no other, even if it may not quite fit the context, is the Polish government's bizarre demand for 1.3 trillion euros in reparations for damage caused by the Second World War. The Polish authors of this demand, and this includes those who believe in the legitimacy of this demand, seem to be suffering from a severe loss of reality. There are clear regulations between the victorious powers regarding the payment of reparations in connection with the

---

[72] https://www.tagesspiegel.de/potsdam/brandenburg/neue-unruhe-um-raffinerie-schwedt-polen-liefert-kein-ol-an-pck-aber-kauft-in-russland-9301376.html

World War. These stipulated in no uncertain terms that all claims by Poland in connection with reparations were to be addressed to the Soviet
Union and were to be settled with it. Further claims against the Federal
Republic of Germany were thus legally excluded. Nevertheless, large areas
with raw material deposits, industrial plants and considerable agricultural
land, which were German before the war and which were initially "German areas under Polish administration" for decades after the war, have

POTSDAM

The Reparations chapter read as follows:

Reparations from Germany[1]

1. Reparation claims of the U.S.S.R. shall be met by removals from the zon
of Germany occupied by the U.S.S.R. and from appropriate Germai
external assets.
2. The U.S.S.R. undertakes to settle the reparation claims of Poland from it
own share of reparations.

Extract from the minutes of the Potsdam Conference.

now been incorporated into Poland. This should correspond to a much
higher value. Perhaps it would be time to precisely quantify the value of
these areas. This should then be set off against the claims of the Poles. Poland would certainly be busy for several generations with the repayment of
the difference in favour of Germany. On the other hand, Poland, for understandable reasons, refrains from making such demands on the Russian
Federation. These would most likely be answered diplomatically by Russia
in an extremely rude manner. How active Poland has been in recent
months, since the start of the war in Ukraine, is shown below. A few
months ago, the author was personally told that high-ranking Lithuanian
politicians had been approached unofficially from the Polish side and had
made an astounding proposal in confidential talks. It was about the recon-

129

veyance of former Lithuanian territories below the Suwalki Gap. The SuwalkiGap (also Suwalki Corridor), in NATO terminology, refers to the area around the border between Lithuania and Poland, which is the only land connection between the Baltic States and the other NATO partners and separates the territory of the Russian exclave Kaliningrad from Belarus. It is named after the town of Suwalki. In return, the Lithuanian government was to be convinced to support a possible advance by Poland against the Russian exclave of Kaliningrad, i.e. the former East Prussia, with Königsberg, as well as an annexation of these territories if necessary. This information dates from August 2022.

At first, it sounds like a bad conspiracy fantasy. However, it is not the first time that the author has been told of such advances by Poland, which has for the past millenium marched into and occupied their neighbours' territories. A further piece of information should be added to this statement obtained through third parties, so that the reader can assess for himself how likely this Polish proposal should be considered. At the end of the 1980s, a gentleman I know well worked for the US-State Department agency in Warsaw. At that time, Polish politicians approached this Lithuanian-born man and presented him with an almost identical proposal. This information is solid, as this source with first-hand information can be considered absolutely reliable. On the one hand, a look at the history books proves that this is not just a conspiracy theory; on the other hand, an interview with Radoslaw Sikorski, Polish Foreign Minister from 2007 to November 2014 and Member of the EU Parliament since 2019, conducted by a Polish radio station on 23rd January 2023, should be mentioned here in conclusion.[73]

---

[73] https://wiadomosci.radiozet.pl/Gosc-Radia-ZET/radoslaw-sikorski-o-jednej-liscie-opozycji-bede-sie-o-to-modlil-23012023

In this interview, he confirmed that Poland was thinking about taking Western Ukraine (formerly known as Galicia) in the first days of the Ukraine war. The current Prime Minister Morawiecki protested and accused Sikorski of Russian propaganda and demanded a correction. To this day, this has not been done. Why? Because it is almost certainly true, and it also makes sense in the geopolitical view of the USA and Poland. This would result in a "win-win situation" for both sides. If Poland were to take western Ukraine, a NATO member would automatically oppose the forward movement of the Russian. Whether the Russians would advance into western Ukraine at this point is highly questionable. America would not have forfeited the entire sphere of influence of Ukraine to Russia in the event of a positive outcome of the war for the Russians. For the Poles, it would be extremely practical, they would be where they have wanted to be again for a long time: in former Polish-occupied territories forfeited to the Soviet Union in 1939. To what extent one could still speak of Ukraine as a functioning state at this point may also be questioned. In such a case, the proposal to place the entire territory under Polish administration would follow as surely as the Amen in the church. The deployment of NATO troops in this area to secure peace might then be even legitimate. Those who now want to counter that Ukraine would certainly not have played along with this do not seem to know that Polish citizens have already been allowed to work in the Ukrainian civil service for a good year and that the Poles see themselves as a peacekeeping force to safeguard Ukrainian (Polish) interests. Ukraine would probably perceive the deployment of Polish troops in western Ukraine not as an occupation, but as military aid against the aggressor Russia, and would present it that way publicly. Before Ukraine falls completely into Russian hands, this scenario would very likely occur; from a strategic and geopolitical point of view, this is the last resort for the West to prevent a complete loss of the geo-strategically important sphere of interest in Ukraine. To dismiss the whole thing as Russian propaganda, as has happened, is specious in view of all this. However, it is relatively clear that the Russian Secret Service has learned of such plans, since the Russians do not live behind the moon either. Reuters reported in April 2022 on this:[74]

"The head of Russia's foreign intelligence service accuses the USA and Poland of planning an invasion of western Ukraine in the event of a Ukrainian defeat and of wanting to install Polish peacekeepers there without a NATO mandate."

The statements are similar. However, it can be assumed that it is a UN Mandate that was meant here. It should be noted, however, that in this case there would be no need for a UN Mandate and even NATO would not have to be involved. The reason for this is that it would be exclusively Polish troops who would enter Western Ukraine – possibly even supported by Lithuanian soldiers. What is the basis for this assumption? On the existence of the "LITPOLUKRBRIG".[75] No, it is not a typo, but the Lithuanian-Polish-Ukrainian brigade. Its foundation has hardly been registered at all in the West. This brigade, which can be up to 4,500 strong in an emergency, was established in 2016. This unit is intended to take over tasks of NATO, the European Union and the UN, but of course for self-defence. Based on this, one can be convinced that Ukraine would see Poland and, to a lesser extent, possibly Lithuania as saviours in need, and would consider every possible option to prevent the Russians from taking

---

[74] https://www.reuters.com/world/russian-spy-chief-says-us-poland-plotting-division-ukraine-2022-04-28/

[75] https://en.wikipedia.org/wiki/Lithuanian%E2%80%93Polish%E2%80%93Ukrainian_Brigade

all of Ukraine. With this brigade, this could even be considered a duty as brothers in arms.

The Baltic States
– wasted chances and opportunities

An important geopolitical region, less for the USA than for Germany, are the Baltic States. Western and pro-Russian foreign policymakers like to ridicule this region for its lack of economic power, but they tend to under-estimate the opportunities and the people, whose mentality is far closer to ours than that of the Russians, for example. As a German, one could make a meaningful contribution in the Baltic States in many ways. The development of economic, but also of cultural relations, are two points of many that still need a lot of improvement. And on closer inspection, the Baltic States are not that small. The three Baltic States together cover an area of 175,000 square kilometres, which is just under half the size of the Federal Republic of Germany, and they have more than 1200 kilometres of coast-line. Unfortunately, Germany did not show the necessary commitment here after 1990, which might have been expected from a historical per-spective. German inactivity was gratefully compensated for by the Scand-inavians. Few people realise that if you have an economic foothold in the Baltic States, it is much easier to gain economic access to Belarus and/or Ukraine. The Latvians, but even more so the Lithuanians, maintain good relations with these countries and a good reputation has always been a good companion. Precisely because the Baltic people are very similar to us in mentality, it is easy to find a common level of communication with them. As a German, it's easy to feel connected to the Baltic States. Especially in the areas along the coast up to Tallinn, Germans have contributed their share to the development over the centuries and thus left a lasting mark on their culture. From Klaipėda (Memel) to Riga and Tallinn (Reval), the German influence cannot be denied or ignored.

The author believes these historical roots are at the same time an obligation to maintain good friendly relations with the Baltic nations in the sense of international understanding as well as to co-operate more closely in political and economic issues. The geopolitical activities of the USA, Poland, and the actions of the current Lithuanian government, some of which can only be described as suicidal, show how endangered the stability of the Baltic States may become. One could assume, at least taking into account a minimum amount of common sense, that every government only has the well-being of its own country and its population in the focus of its activities. That this does not necessarily apply to Germany has already been recognised by some – though still too few. That Lithuania now has a similar problem, which will, however, lead more quickly to national dissolution as in the case of the Federal Republic of Germany, since time is obviously of the essence, is new. So new, in fact, that the Lithuanian people have been caught stone-cold by it in their own country. The extent to which Lithuania has become a pawn in the game of geopolitical interests and how little respect its own government obviously has for its country is shown by some extremely disturbing activities of the Lithuanian government. Lithuania pursued a strategy of neutrality during the Second World War, but it did not pay off for them. Today, on the other hand, the strategy is to align and submit to the strongest partner, from whom it hopes to gain protection from an overpowering neighbour that is perceived as hostile. Previous chapters described the Eastern Europeans' fear of the Russians and outlined where this fear comes from. In connection with the Baltic States, it is also important to explain why the Balts have a particular aversion to Russia. After the invasion of the Red Army and the occupation of Lithuania, 250,000 Lithuanians alone were deported by the Soviets during and after the war. Thousands were taken into forests and cruelly tortured and killed. Because of the partisan war waged by the Lithuanians, who courageously fought back against the occupying forces, the Soviets deported entire villages to prevent the inhabitants from supporting these resistance fighters. In this context, it is also worth mentioning that this partisan struggle in Lithuania continued until 1953. The reason for this was mainly that American and British secret services promised support to the Lithuanians again and again, motivating them to continue the fight against the Soviets. The truth is, however, that this promised support never materialised: the Lithuanians were burnt out in the interests of the USA and Great Britain. Estonians and Latvians, too, had their culture and language ruthlessly suppressed and with similar deportations during the Soviet era. The Kremlin no longer wants to know about the war crimes committed by the Soviet Union at that time. For example, the 18,000 Latvians who were deported in 1941, one week before the German attack, for security reasons, as it was feared that they might collaborate with the Germans. Very few of them came back. What the Latvians particularly resent about the Soviets and what has a lasting effect was the Russification of Latvia through the resettlement there of tens of thousands of ethnic Russians. At the time, they were required as workers to build up large-scale local industry.

Back to current politics in Lithuania: Let's look at how the USA is busy whispering things to the Lithuanian government here as well, the implementation of which is anything but beneficial for Lithuania. Lithuania, however, seems to be trying hard to prove to its supposed partner, but definitive hegemon, how loyal it is, overlooking the consequences and problems that could, or will, result for its own people and state. The whole thing started with the full-bodied recognition of Taiwan, being the first state in Europe to send a signal to the Chinese leadership. China was visibly impressed and terminated economic relations with Lithuania and in turn imposed additional economic sanctions against it. Lithuania took another step towards its downfall by prohibiting Belarus from transporting potassium inland to the Baltic port of Klaipėda, where it was shipped all over the world and especially to China. This instantly deprived the port of about 30 per cent of its revenue. The result was short-time work and lay-offs. The crowning act of foreign policy hara-kiri, however, was the blocking of land transit for Russian trains to the exclave of Königsberg (Kaliningrad Oblast). A more than daring act, considering that the transit agreement was an essential component for Russia's recognition of Lithuanian independence.[76] [77] It is therefore not surprising that the Russians clearly reacted by no longer officially recognising Lithuania's state borders.1 That this action could have led to a rapid and tangible escalation in the region had to be clear to each of the parties involved from the outset. So why are such decisions made and, above all, by whom? However, provoking an escalation with the feared big neighbour, a nuclear power, is certainly not part of the toolkit of a Lithuanian politician who wants to protect the sovereignty and freedom of his nation. So the only conclusion that can be drawn is that some people in the Lithuanian government are not acting in the best interests of their own nation. They allow themselves to be manipulated and thus act on behalf of those who consider an escalation in East-

[76] https://www.rnd.de/politik/kaliningrad-moskau-stellt-litauens-grenzen-infrage-2R5YE6WNMX4HONFUGJU6OQ.html

[77] https://georgiatoday.ge/growing-tensions-between-russia-and-the-baltic-states-the-kremlin-threatens-nato-members/

ern Europe useful and are largely responsible for it. Lithuania has meanwhile exchanged its own national colours for those of Ukraine on some official buildings and official websites. Solidarity in all honour, but this is going too far for a large part of the population, as can be seen from comments in the social media. But does that mark the end of national self-sacrifice? Not at all: Recently, the Prime Minister of Lithuania travelled to Warsaw and revealed her great sympathy for Poland and her Polish roots. Instead of Lithuanian, Polish was spoken more frequently in the family. The astonishment of large parts of the Lithuanian population was certainly great, since this was not known to anyone before the elections and was not publicised by the press. The plans for the "Intermarium" mentioned in the previous chapter are now relatively officially discussed and supported by the Lithuanian government. This time, Poland seems to have chosen the right time with the right geopolitical framework conditions, or perhaps even to have been given them. Everything that is currently developing geopolitically in Eastern Europe, when put into context, increasingly gives the impression of being planned through. In the knowledge of the geopolitical disturbing fires and the fact that the Baltic States would be severely endangered in the event of a Russian offensive, the question arises whether this was not planned as a possible scenario from the very beginning. Thus, it is within the bounds of probability that the Baltic States should be regarded as a military buffer zone, with the same poor prospects as the Federal Republic of Germany had in the days of the Cold War. An ally who disregards the interests of his own allies without scruples or who asserts his own interests through the use of manipulation, lies and sabotage to the detriment of the allies is not an ally; he is the proverbial cuckoo in his own nest and will not hesitate to sacrifice his own allies, on the geopolitical battlefield, for his own benefit.

Could the war in Ukraine have been prevented?

Preventing or ending a war means, first and foremost, talking. "Those who talk to each other do not shoot at each other," said former German Foreign Minister Hans Dietrich Genscher. This communication, which prevailed between East and West for decades and ultimately also secured peace in Europe, has deteriorated over the last 25 years. That this is mainly due to the expansionist policy of the USA and its obvious proxy organisation NATO, and their decisive influence on the foreign policy of some European states, we have seen from the previous chapters. We have also been able to establish that the Russians are not the proverbial innocent bystanders. The Russian side has often acted clumsily or reacted in a way that encouraged escalation rather than preventing it. It remains to be said that Russia has been left little room to develop its own spheres of interest in Eastern Europe. The pressure built up by NATO's eastward expansion, especially with regard to Ukraine, and in connection with the construction of the missile defence shield, was enormous. A German proverb says "As one calls into the forest, so it resounds out", indicating that certain behaviour is certain to provoke a certain reaction. You also cannot get indefinitely close to a wild animal in the wild if it has no means of retreat, and provoking it when it has no way out will force it to attack. This parable may not appeal to some, but it brings what is happening in Eastern Europe down to a simple and understandable denominator. The Russian bear has been cornered in many ways over the past 25 years. This is not to say, however, that Russian action has been legitimate or appropriate in all cases. On the Russian side, as described earlier, there have been numerous failures in terms of understanding with Eastern European states and foreign policy détente in Eastern Europe after the end of the Soviet Union.

The strategic necessity to become active against the geopolitics of the USA on its own doorstep was obligatory for Russia. Unfortunately, Russia obviously understood too late that a thick skin and sitting out any problems that might arise will not lead to the desired result. Russia should at least have gone on the offensive diplomatically. Talks should have been held with the immediate neighbouring states. An understanding of wrongs committed and ways of redress would have created further options that would have been equally beneficial for both sides. Assurances of territorial integrity and military non-aggression pacts would have been a clear signal to the Russian Federation's western neighbours that the former Soviet republics have nothing to fear from Russia. This would also have allowed Russia to put a stop to the Americans' encroachment into their spheres of interest. The easy game of the USA and NATO to implement their geostrategic plans and to turn every country except Belarus against Russia is based on the circumstances of uncertainty as to how Russia would behave towards them. Thus, the only option left for Russia's neighbouring states was to flee into the arms of NATO and thus into the clutches of the USA and its foreign policy built on self-interest and hegemony.

Current developments in this conflict make it abundantly clear that both sides have little interest in negotiating. In the case of Ukraine, it is obvious why. Fuelled by the daily rhetoric of hold-out slogans, as well as the arms supplies from the West instrumentalised by the USA, Ukrainians actually believe in a victory over Russia, including a reconquest of the Crimean Peninsula. A question that first arises fundamentally here is how arms deliveries are supposed to shorten the war or even create peace in this situation? Especially in a situation where, despite the weapons supplied to Ukraine, the war enemy Russia still has a greater quantity of all the necessary materials for waging war than Ukraine. That the West, through aggressive expansionist geopolitics in Eastern Europe, bears a substantial share of the responsibility for this avoidable tragedy is clear to anyone who has studied this subject in depth or read this far. When two people are arguing and beating each other with their fists, it is not very helpful to put a knife in the hand of the person who is probably the loser and think that this will settle the conflict. As expected, the other will also arm itself and adapt its strategy. Similarly, if knives are exchanged for firearms, missiles, or tanks. It will go on until one of the two is dead, both are so injured that it is no longer possible to continue fighting, or the weaker one gives up. If the ratio of combatants is three to one or worse, the result would quickly be on the table. However, if I now support the numerically and equipment-wise inferior with weapons and strategic information, the picture distorts considerably and the first effect, without achieving a result, is the significant prolongation of the conflict. Based on this fact, it is irresponsible on the part of the USA and some NATO countries such as Poland or Lithuania to put fantasies about the conquest of Crimea and a victory over Russia into Ukraine's head without having even a hint of a real strategic argument as to how this goal can actually be achieved without completely bleeding Ukraine dry. Sooner or later, it will become necessary to intervene with foreign troops sent to Ukraine in order to achieve such goals. This, however, would be predestined to cause a conflagration. Geopolitics is being pursued here at the expense of tens of thousands, if not hundreds of thousands, of Ukrainian soldiers and civilians, which is neither directly nor indirectly in Ukraine's interest. Ukraine is being used as a proxy for the USA and Poland against Russia. While this will marginally weaken Russia, it will not lead to the desired outcome of victory over Russia or the Polish desire to break up the Russian Federation.[78]

---

[78] https://responsiblestatecraft.org/2023/03/24/why-pushing-for-the-break-up-of-russia-is-absolute-folly/

It is in some ways revealing when the US, NATO, and the EU talk about peace, but everything they do leads to worsening the situation and prolonging the suffering of the people in Ukraine. Every step the West has taken since the outbreak of the war has been a step further to escalation. From the beginning, there has not been a single serious diplomatic push by the USA, the EU, or a single European state, except for Turkey, to try to resolve this conflict at the negotiating table.

On 28th February 2022, talks began in Belarus to settle the hostilities but were adjourned without result after five hours of talks. In the second round of negotiations on 3rd of March, agreement was only reached on humanitarian corridors for the evacuation of the civilian population and a possible temporary ceasefire in these areas. A third round of negotiations took place on March 7th, which basically did not result in any further improvement of the situation. Only a logistical improvement for the humanitarian corridors could be negotiated. These talks were followed by a meeting of Foreign Ministers Sergei Lavrov and Dmytro Kuleba on March 10th. The Russian side's demand envisaged Ukraine's neutrality and apparently complete disarmament. This, in turn, would amount to abandonment, which Ukrainian Foreign Minister Kuleba unequivocally rejected. As a result, Russia rejected a 24-hour ceasefire to evacuate Mariupol. In a fourth round of negotiations from March 14th to 17th, Russia demanded neutrality from the neighbouring country along Austrian or Swiss lines. Thereupon, Ukraine demanded security guarantees from Western states. The media later reported that Ukraine rejected neutrality and that the demand for security guarantees was linked to further arms deliveries. In response to Russia's demand for denazification of the Ukrainian state apparatus, Ukrainian Foreign Minister Dmytro Kuleba smugly tweeted that instead of the "denazification" demanded by Moscow, he was calling for "deputisation": Russia should be cut off internationally from any influence in politics, economics, energy, culture and other areas[79] (Basically a continuation of the pre-1991 Cold War).

However, anyone who uses such language during peace talks as the highest diplomatic representative of the country under attack need not be surprised that negotiations may not have the desired success. Volodymyr Zelenskyj said in connection with the talks, "We all want peace and victory as soon as possible". This statement, too, does not quite fit with peace negotiations, at the end of which a compromise of some kind should be found. All compromise proposals were rejected by Ukraine. The last negotiations of this kind took place in Istanbul on 29th March 2023. Roman Abramovich acted as mediator. Although the Russian proposal for Ukraine's neutrality had been rejected a good two weeks earlier, it was now proposed by Ukraine itself as part of a ten-point plan. Ukraine was prepared to renounce joining NATO and to accept a ban on foreign military bases on Ukrainian territory. However, this was again made conditional. Reliable security guarantees were demanded from members of the UN Security Council, Turkey, Poland, and Germany.

The issue of Crimea, Donbass, and Luhansk would have been left out of this agreement for the time being. The withdrawal of Russian troops to positions before 23rd of February 2022 would also have been part of this agreement. It is interesting that at this point, none of the Western states mentioned was willing to give this security guarantee to Ukraine. On the contrary, one could see in the media that the USA and the UK in particular were constantly encouraging Ukraine to make further demands and

---

[79] https://www.tagesschau.de/ausland/europa/ukraine-russland-verhandlungen-111.html

promised unwavering military support. The Israeli mediation attempt in mid-June 2022 also failed, although Naftali Bennet was successful in persuading Vladimir Putin to make concessions. This important attempt to bring about a ceasefire was also prevented by people like Boris Johnson, who publicly called for no concessions to be made to Russia. When asked by a journalist if it was the West that blocked a ceasefire, Bennet replied, "Basically yes".[80]

Germany, as Russia's close economic partner, could have acted positively as a mediator on the Russian president, just as Bennet did. Unfortunately, no attempt was made to act in this direction. Instead, the rhetoric of all the German left-wing government representatives was more about unilaterally offering Ukraine hope and assurances of military support, rather than working towards a peaceful resolution of the conflict. Anyone in Germany who suggested this, or intended to make a move in this direction, was publicly pilloried, indiscriminately branded a "Russia sympathizer" or "Putin friend". It was made clear to everyone in this country that diplomacy and peace negotiations are not really wanted. The USA and Poland could have influenced Ukraine accordingly if they had actually wanted to do so. Attempts to initiate multilateral mediation, possibly by involving various credible, neutral negotiators, were not made. Attempts at mediation on the Turkish side were registered rather casually by the West.

If one had really wanted to prevent such a confrontation as the present one, then the way NATO/USA and the EU have dealt with Ukraine over the last 15 years should have been completely different. Aware that Russia's red line is precisely Ukraine, they should have worked towards a neutral,

[80] https://www.tagesschau.de/ausland/europa/ukraine-russland-verhandlungen-111.html

non-aligned status for Ukraine by respecting the existing Russian-Ukrainian treaties accordingly and giving them the urgently needed consideration in geopolitical activities. The gradual "drawing" of Ukraine into the Western sphere of interest, militarily as well as economically and politically, was a consequence of mistakes, provided that peacekeeping and the avoidance of war had actually been the goal in mind. However, since it cannot be assumed in such long-lasting and momentous matters that a "few mistakes" were simply made over the years, it must inevitably be assumed that this was a deliberate act.

Russia, to put it bluntly, allowed itself to be provoked. The war that began on 24th of February 2022 could still have been prevented at the time. It should not be forgotten, however, that Ukrainian President Volodymyr Zelenskyj had already made demands for weapons to NATO before the outbreak of the war and even threatened to declare the Budapest Memorandum invalid. Here is the wording:

"I am initiating consultations within the framework of the Budapest Memorandum and have instructed the Foreign Minister to convene them. If the meeting fails again or if no security guarantees for Ukraine are granted, Kiev reserves the right to declare the Budapest Memorandum invalid. Then all package solutions reached in 1994 will be called into question. "[81] This would also mean that Kiev would have renounced the Nuclear Non-Proliferation Treaty. The Secretary of Ukraine's National Security and Defence Council, Alexei Danilov, had declared at the end of 2021 that Kiev's renunciation of nuclear weapons should be compensated for by the delivery of "offensive weapons". Now the word "offensive weapons" catches one's eye with

---

[81] https://snanews.de/20220219/selenski-droht-mit-revision-von-beschluss-zum-verzicht-kiews-auf-atomwaffen-5434948.html

such a statement.[82] Why does Ukraine need offensive weapons? If it feels threatened as a country by Russia and also wants to become a NATO member urgently because of this, then defensive weapons would be the wise choice, unless the actual intentions are somewhat different than officially presented. This, in turn, would cast a very different light on the actions of Ukrainian troops in the east of the country. Soberly considered and taking into account all the facts gathered, it appears that this confrontation could not have been avoided sooner or later. The reasons for this are obvious. The Russian interests and the demands Russia derived from them were and are being ignored by Ukraine, the USA, and NATO. Incidentally, the same applies to the economic interests of Germany, which for decades has been supplied with large quantities of cheap and relatively clean energy from Russia and previously from the Soviet Union. Russian submissions to the European Court of Human Rights and the UN General Assembly regarding the continued human rights violations in the east of the country, which Ukrainian government troops are accused of against the Russian population, did not result in any significant reaction. The Minsk Agreement has not been mutually respected. Angela Merkel's statement on it was understandably extremely disturbing for Russia. She indicated in an interview that this Agreement only served the purpose of buying Ukraine time to rearm militarily. Concluding such agreements under false pretences would be a particularly serious breach of trust and also a breach of international law.[83]

European interests play only a subordinate role in this complex process of upheaval. Essentially, it is about implementing the goals of the globalists and the neocons in the USA. The USA wants to gain access to the "rim-

[82] https://snanews.de/20220219/selenski-droht-mit-revision-von-beschluss-zum-verzicht-kiews-auf-atomwaffen-5434948.html
[83] https://www.globaltimes.cn/page/202212/1281708.shtml

land" (peripheral zone around the heartland) at all costs, in order to further expand its own power and influence over the heartland from there. If necessary, the players, accomplices and useful idiots are gladly made to believe that they are fighting for the people and the motherland, for sovereignty and democracy, although the only interests that really matter are those of the USA and, secondarily, those of its closest helpers. It is extremely tragic what is happening in Ukraine: The people are literally being burnt to death in the name of interest-driven globalist policies, but believe themselves to be fighting for their freedom and independence. This sounds exceedingly "conspiracy-theoretical", but as announced at the beginning of the book, the necessary facts, comments, or quotations are also provided for all statements, and so also here. The following is a quote from a 1993 Open Letter by billionaire alleged philanthropist George Soros, which is exposing and which anyone who can afford to have any kind of opinion about this conflict should know.

George Soros

"The United States should not be called upon to act as the world's policeman. When it does act, it does so in co-operation with others. Moreover, the combination of large numbers of people from Eastern Europe with NATO's technical capabilities would greatly enhance the military potential of the partnership by reducing the risk of body bags for NATO countries, which is the main obstacle to their readiness to act. This is a viable alternative to the looming global disorder".[84]

[84] https://cms.zerohedge.com/s3/files/inline-images/2023-01-23_07-55-26.jpg?itok=bAB_ztPE

Soros notes that NATO countries have no interest in "body bags" but that this problem can be eliminated by allowing Eastern Europeans to fill this role. What Soros describes here with frightening sobriety has unfolded exactly as he predicted with regard to the war in Ukraine. Armed with high quality NATO weapons, Ukrainian soldiers are actively moving against Russia, which Soros had already feared would develop into a nationalist nation that would oppose the global order he propagated in 1993.

With this in mind, it is far easier to understand why Hungary, with its government under Prime Minister Viktor Orban, expelled George Soros's Foundation network, headed by the Open Society Foundation, even though Orban and his party ,Fidesz MPSC' ("Hungarian Civic Federation") owe a great deal to George Soros.[85]

Protecting national interests and state stability remains a priority in Hungary. Instead of constantly criticising Hungary, Europe should take an example of how to proceed in order to protect its own interests against external influences. It is important to know that the Open Society Foundation's network of foundations, partners, and projects is spread over more than 120 countries worldwide.[86]

These are suspected of intervening massively in social events and political issues in numerous countries, on various continents. This is done by specially trained and financed activists who create allegedly social or liberal "opposition movements" and use them to spread their ideologies in society.

---

[85] https://www.dw.com/de/wie-george-soros-zum-feindbild-wurde/a-53572731
[86] https://www.opensocietyfoundations.org/george-soros

In some countries, such non-governmental organisations (NGOs) can even be used to prepare revolutions and coups. We have already read about this in the chapter on the NeoCons. These activities are officially justified with freedom or peace initiatives, promotion of democracy, anti-racism, support of immigration (in deliberate disregard of asylum laws), or even environmental protection measures and the deadly argument of "saving the planet".

All too often, the fact that foreign NGOs or their middlemen are behind suddenly emerging demonstrations and opposition movements, as well as radical subversion efforts, is not even widely known. However, very little of what is played out for us on the "world stage" happens by chance or arises of its own accord. Unfortunately, the activities of Soros organisations, or other NGOs, are rarely, if ever, critically questioned by the Western media. And if they should ask in an interview, they are satisfied with a simple evasive answer, although other sources speak a clear language and give a completely different picture.[87]

Russia without an alternative?

The frequently heard statement that the Russian leadership had no choice but to attack Ukraine must be relegated to the land of legends. A few pages earlier, reasons were already listed that contradict this statement. There was no immediate need for action on Russia's part that could justify such a far-reaching and destructive act. Neither could this attack be described as

[87] https://www.welt.de/politik/ausland/article244158213/Mark-Malloch-Brown-Wir-sehen-ein-Scheitern-des-aktuellen-Modells-von-Regierungsfuehrung.html#Comments;

pre-emptive, nor was Russia's territorial integrity at risk at any time. Russia caused something of a surprise with its attack on Ukraine. Many assumed that after Vladimir Putin recognised the independence of the Luhansk and Donetsk regions on 21st February 2022, the troop presence in these areas would be increased to ensure the security of the new people's republics. It is possible that Russia's decision was also accompanied by a certain spontaneity. From the beginning, Russia's military action gave a poorly co-ordinated impression. Reports from various sources told of a lack of information among officers and units, who initially believed it was an exercise. The relatively quick onset of the lack of supplies could have been a further indication that Ukraine's ability to defend itself was underestimated and that it believed it could already bring about a decision with the material at hand. One should not forget that Ukraine had the second-largest army in Europe at the outbreak of the war, despite only having a population of 43 million. Perhaps they also underestimated the West's willingness and ability to supply Ukraine with vast quantities of weapons. There may have been other reasons that led the Kremlin to take this drastic step. Before we turn to the official accessible arguments, we should ask an intermediate question that may also provide us with part of the answer to the question we have just asked.

Since we have established that many of the geopolitical strategies of the USA are of a long-term nature, we must inevitably ask ourselves whether the Russian Federation is now or was at an earlier time engaged in similar geopolitics, or whether the Soviet Union was. In this context, it has first become clear that Russia, with certain conspicuous behaviour towards its neighbours, especially with regard to domestic political developments after 1990, has not sought confidence-building measures and an active policy of détente.

The Russian Federation accuses the West, mostly justifiably, of merely wanting to stall for time to arm Ukraine with certain activities. It is common knowledge that Ukraine was already supplied with weapons by the West before 2014. After the referendum in Crimea and Moscow's subsequent annexation, these efforts were stepped up again, and Ukraine publicly called for increased deliveries of offensive weapons.

To what extent might Russia also have devised a very long-term strategy that was at least recognised or perceived in this way in the West, and was also designed to buy time? In order to pursue this question, we have to look 40 years into the past and consider the situation of the Soviet Union at that time in a little more detail.

The Soviet Union had not been able to keep up with the West economically and militarily since the mid-1980s at the latest. Their infrastructure was hopelessly outdated. Economic growth had been declining for some time. The main problem was that the quality of the products no longer met international standards, and important exports to generate foreign currency were missing. Due to the isolation from the West, largely due to sanctions, and socialist mismanagement, essential goods were missing, which in turn would have been necessary to keep up with progress in the West. What we see today in Ukraine was also very pronounced in the Soviet Union: corruption. The Soviet Union also had to struggle with an inefficient shadow economy that largely eluded control and gave rise to social and economic "parallel worlds", as existed in many socialist countries.

This was of course accompanied by another major issue. Scientific research could no longer achieve any significant successes due to the economy of scarcity. In many areas, it no longer corresponded to the state of general development. Especially in the field of high technology, the Soviet Union could no longer keep up with the West. This was particularly evident in the military sector. The costs for their completely outdated arsenal were immense, while its effectiveness was at a low level. The entire military material was completely outdated. Tanks, ships, and submarines had to be partially decommissioned because operational safety could no longer be guaranteed and repair was no longer possible due to a lack of components. The immense costs of the Soviet-Afghan war, starting in December 1979, put an additional strain on the budget. Here, of course, the USA saw a decisive opportunity to engage the Soviet Union in a war of attrition and demonstrably supported the radical Islamic forces with weapons and ammunition. This massive war of attrition further depleted the Soviet military apparatus and cost many soldiers their lives.

In 1985, Mikhail Gorbachev came to power as the new Secretary of State and promised to end the war. The Soviet leadership came to the realisation that the war could not be won, and searched desperately for a way to end it and evacuate without losing face. With the realisation that this war had no chance of success against a theoretically inferior opponent, the leading people in the Kremlin became even more pensive than they already were with regard to their economy and technology deficits. The lack of possibilities to develop and produce new, better weapons showed that the current political course had no chance of success. A decisive change in strategy was needed. Gorbachev knew that the reforms had to be fundamental and that solutions had to be put on the table quickly. With Gorbachev, the two concepts of "glasnost" (openness/transparency) and subsequent "perestroika" (transformation) gained momentum. The aim was to restructure and modernise the social, political and economic system of the Soviet Union. The first steps were taken towards freedom of the press and freedom of opinion, and glasnost was to mark the beginning of a democratisation process in 1986.

Perestroika took off in 1988 with the aim of reforming socialism. In principle, the aim was to have free elections and to give socialism a democratic face through the separation of powers and the introduction of the rule of law. In this way, they wanted to stabilise the entire Eastern bloc. Of course, this policy of détente was also pursued in external affairs. In 1987, for example, they worked towards ending the Cold War. Gorbachev and Ronald Reagan signed the INF Treaty, which provided for the destruction of all ground and land-based cruise missiles with shorter and medium ranges (500 to 5500 kilometres). In addition, the Soviet leadership decided to drastically reduce financial support to communist rebels in Africa and Latin America. Perhaps one of the most significant and important steps for the Soviet Union's approach was the abolition of the Brezhnev Doctrine. This doctrine provided for the restriction of the sovereignty of all socialist countries within the Soviet Union's sphere of power. The main thesis is:

"The interests and sovereignty of individual socialist states find their limits in the interests and security of the entire socialist system."

The final communiqué of the Warsaw Treaty Political Consultative Committee in Bucharest on 7th July 1989 states:

"That each people itself determines the destiny of its country and has the right to choose for itself the socio-political and economic system, the state order, which it considers suitable for itself. There is not only one standard for the or-

ganisation of society ... No country may dictate the course of events within another country, no one may arrogate to himself the role of judge or arbiter."

On 7th December 1988, Gorbachev had announced a significant reduction in Soviet troops in Eastern Europe. All the measures listed had three main objectives:

1. The significant reduction of the expenditure of the Soviet state apparatus, which was no longer in any position to maintain the old system, and

2. the opening of the Eastern bloc and Russia towards the West.

3. credibly presenting to the West that from now on peace and understanding would be pursued instead of intimidation and deterrence.

All these were important prerequisites for rehabilitating the country economically, technologically and militarily in a long-term strategy. Only in this way was it possible to bring it back to a level that could cope with competition at all levels, but also with a possible confrontation with the West.

The Eastern bloc disintegrated in the years after 1989; Poland and Hungary made a start here. But that was initially a small price to pay for the fact that these and other measures created a way to obtain urgently needed foreign currency and Western technology. Investors from the West were not long in coming, either. Those who see perestroika as an act of pure charity and the desire for peace and friendship on the part of the Soviet Union fail to recognise the predicament and strategic considerations of those in power at the time, and especially Mikhail Gorbachev.

However, if one considers perestroika not only as a sign of peaceful change in the Eastern Bloc, but as a geopolitical method and strategy, then one must pay the highest respect to those who devised it. Ultimately, perestroika allowed the Soviet Union and its successor, the Russian Federation, to consolidate economically, technologically and militarily without being exposed to significant foreign policy pressure during this period. However, decades of socialist mismanagement cannot be completely remedied in half the time, and so there were still considerable deficits, especially in the industrial and military sectors.

Boris Yeltsin's tenure as Russian leader, 1991 to 1999, was a slip in planning. Russia fell into considerable economic, social and political difficulties. The broad masses were extremely dissatisfied with the new situation; the sale of formerly state-owned enterprises and raw material deposits to private oligarchs assumed state-threatening proportions. But when Vladimir Putin took office, the strategy of structural regeneration could be effectively continued. Putin began, probably prematurely, to flex the muscles that had not yet been sufficiently built up militarily. The intervention in Georgia, in 2008, did not pose any significant problems for the Russian army, but it did show the trained eye that the Russian army did not yet have the optimal equipment and operational strength in some areas. One example of this was the deployment of Russian long-range bombers against Georgia, because the necessary short-range missiles with conventional warheads were not yet available.[88]

---

[88] https://www.deutschlandfunk.de/russisches-armeegeraet-ist-hoffnungslos-ueberaltert-100.html

If we look at 2014 and the conflict between Russia and Ukraine, which was already smouldering at that time, one thing becomes clear: the political situation was already almost identical to today. Ukraine wanted to become a member of NATO and the EU at any cost, prompted and supported by the USA. The West was already supplying weapons to Ukraine, and Russian-speaking minorities were being attacked by Ukrainian ultra-nationalist Nazi squads chanting anti-Russian slogans. The openly Nazi-affiliated Svoboda party had become part of the Ukrainian government. If the Russian army had been able to do so at the time, an attack like the one on 24th February 2022 would most likely have taken place then. So, for the time being, the smaller interim solution was opted for and Crimea was annexed in order to permanently secure at least the strategically important access to the Black Sea. One can only assume that Moscow feared that incalculable decisions on the Ukrainian side would expose it in the short term to a cancellation of the Russian-Ukrainian naval treaty, which provided for the stationing of the Russian Black Sea Fleet until 2042. This is, of course, a theory, but observing the military action and the military material used by the Russian armed forces, such a thesis suggests itself. The Russian army was not yet ready for an operation of such magnitude. That is why it refrained from doing so in 2014. From the Russian point of view, they were now possibly in a dilemma in 2022: should they wait longer and thus continue to watch Ukraine being rearmed by the West and, if necessary, be caught cold by Ukraine's admission to NATO? This would indeed have had the consequence that Russia would have irretrievably lost its most important sphere of interest and a buffer state between itself and the NATO members. As a consequence, the deployment of NATO troops of the ‚NATO Forward Presence' would have been likely. That Russia could not take this risk must be seen as understandable, at least from the Russian point of view.

155

If we look again at the Soviet-Afghan war and its prehistory, we see that the Soviet Union supported the government of the previously proclaimed Democratic Republic of Afghanistan. This came to power after the so-called "Saur Revolution", i.e. the revolution in the month of the bull, on 27th April 1978. It was carried out by members of the communist DVPA (People's Democratic Party of Afghanistan). This was an attempt by the communists to re-establish their position in the country. It has been proven that the Soviet Union had no influence on the coup that was carried out. After the coup, however, massive power struggles again emerged within the DVPA. The situation within the new government thus became steadily more confusing. The attempts to subject the state to a radical and also brutal transformation also caused massive resistance to the government. Concerned that this communist government might lose control, Soviet troops invaded Afghanistan on 25th December 1979. The Soviet intervention was immediately condemned internationally by the West.

An Islamic coalition was formed against the Soviet occupiers, which received increasing international recognition. In this context, one often reads about "conservative" mujahideen. This means nothing other than that these jihadist resistance fighters adhered to traditional and thus radical Islam. The USA supported them with money and arms supplies, thus causing a drastic prolongation of the war. Once again, the double standards of the USA came to the fore, seizing the opportunity to wage a proxy war with the aim of weakening the Soviet Union. Support was given to those who, a little over ten years later, were declared the worst enemy on earth, the Taliban. The end result was the same: after 20 years of war in Afghanistan, which began in 2001, the USA and its Western allies had to leave Afghanistan with their tails between their legs, leaving behind more than

156

a billion dollars worth of military equipment and the Taliban in government.

In conclusion, apart from its expansionist phase at the beginning, the Soviet Union has pursued geopolitical ventures within its means. In the 1980s, the possibilities of the Soviet Union to exert geopolitical influence were reduced to zero due to dwindling economic and financial resources and also due to a reduced military power. The high military expenditure in Afghanistan had literally bled the Soviet Union dry in many areas. The current, progressive consolidation of the Russian Federation indicates that it wants to extricate itself from this situation. Since Russia will not allow itself to be degraded by the USA as a "regional power", it is trying in the meantime, similar to China, to assert itself through economic geopolitics and thus, in the absence of a powerful army or out of conviction, to expand its spheres of interest in this way.

But now back to the arguments that we have encountered with recurring regularity in the media. First there is the denazification argument put forward by Russia. However, this does not give them the right to invade a sovereign state. As unpleasant as this problem is, it remains a purely Ukrainian one that requires an internal solution and does not allow for further delay. To be clear, Ukraine does indeed have a neo-Nazi and extremist issue and that this is not just Russian propaganda. In recent years, before the outbreak of war in 2022, corresponding images were published several times in the press.[89] [90] [91]

---

[89] http://www.jg-berlin.org/beitraege/details/nazikollaborateur-als-neuer-held-der-ukraine-i276d-2010-04-01.html

[90] https://www.focus.de/politik/videos/asow-miliz-deutsche-neo-nazis-kaempfen-offenbar-in-ukrainischer-soeldner-truppe_id_7844314.html

[91] https://www.reuters.com/article/us-cohen-ukraine-commentary-idUSKBN1GV2TY

Whereas in Germany every small "c" conservative and/or critically thinking citizen is labelled as a right-wing "extremist" or "Nazi" and may be freely called one, things are seen much more loosely with regard to Ukraine. Here, obvious neo-Nazi structures that use symbolism that is classified as anti-constitutional in Germany are at best rarely mentioned by German media, downgraded to the level of right-wing extremist or below, in order to preserve the appearance of the rule of law and order in Ukraine. In 2014, this happened with some activists of the Ukrainian Svoboda party who used clear insignia of National Socialism and yet were elected to political office. In the case of the Azov Regiment, too, swastikas, SS runes, wolf fishing rods and other symbols are used that could not be clearer in their message.[92] Nevertheless, the government made the regiment part of the Ukrainian National Guard. This in turn reports directly to the Ministry of the Interior. These people are publicly spreading hatred of Russia and fuelling the mood against Russians in Ukraine, who have been subjected to massive repression and persecution, including mistreatment and organised murder, since 2014. But that's not all, because hatred against Jews and Germans is also propagated here. However, all this does not seem to stop the German President Frank-Walter Steinmeier from having his picture taken together with these people and from cooperating on a political level.[93] If we now recall that this very President congratulated Iran on the 40th anniversary of the Islamic Revolution in a telegram that neither addressed the human rights situation nor criticised the financing of terrorist organisations such as Hamas and Hezbollah, such behaviour is not only disconcerting and unworthy of a President, it is also a slap in the

---

[92] https://www.handelsblatt.com/politik/deutschland/chefredakteur-in-der-kritik-eklat-im-zdf-fernsehrat-wegen-ukraine-bericht/10755886.html

[93] https://www.dw.com/de/zwischen-hoffen-und-bangen-in-kiew/a-17448315

face of the Israelis, who are exposed to constant threats of annihilation by Iran.

And the politics since 2015 can hardly be surpassed in its duplicity. Politicians affirm the unrestricted right of the State of Israel to exist and invoke the protection of the Jewish faith in Germany. On the other hand, migrants whose faith is 95 percent Islamic have been pouring into the country since 2015, and these people are allowed to publicly chant "Death to the Jews" with impunity at demonstrations. Instead of seriously addressing this problem, the political right spectrum and the Alternative for Germany as a political party are bizarrely accused of fuelling hatred of Jews in Germany. The neo-Nazis of the Azov Regiment also make no secret of who their enemies are. On the one hand, there are the Russians, who must be driven out of the country; on the other hand, they also see the EU as an enemy.[94] An essential question that automatically arises is where do these people draw the line? If the EU is their declared enemy, one must assume that the European member states of this community are also seen as enemies. The irrational agitation against Germans seems to reinforce this assumption. It is relatively obvious that this rampant nationalism or national chauvinism is something that has been superimposed and forced on a healthy Ukrainian patriotism. The Ukrainian masses are being misused here under false pretences for wholly unpatriotic ends and interests of foreigners.

The CIA and MI6 (the British foreign intelligence service) connection to Nazis in Ukraine goes back to the end of the Second World War. Organisations such as the OUN-B (Organisation of Ukrainian Nationalists – Stepan Bandera wing) collaborated with the National Socialists and the

---

[94] https://www.20min.ch/story/ukraine-setzt-neo-nazis-gegen-separatisten-ein-717051112073

Third Reich during the Second World War and tried to expand their influence in Ukraine during the war. Stepan Bandera was a convinced fascist and leader of the OUN-B and is revered in Ukraine today in widespread government and military circles. Mykola Lebed, Stepan Bandera's right-hand man, was recruited by the CIA after the war. Stepan Bandera, on the other hand, was recruited by MI6. The operatives of the OUN-B settled for the most part in America. In the mid-1980s, the Reagan administration was riddled with UCCA members (UCCA - Ukrainian Congress Committee of America). President Reagan even personally received Yaroslav Stetsko, the Banderist leader who oversaw the massacre of 7,000 Jews in Lviv (Lemberg), at the White House in 1983.[95] In 1998, the era of the OUN-B ended with Lebed's death. However, the idea lived on in the UCCA and steadily gained political influence in the USA. After the fall of Yanukovych's government, the UCCA helped organise rallies in cities across the USA in support of the Euro-Maidan demonstations in Kiev.

The European Security Academy (ESA), which is a Polish private company offering training programmes for security, law enforcement and military personnel, has since 2016 provided special forces training to a large group from Ukraine, composed at least in part of Azov veterans, current members of the Azov movement and other National Socialist or fascist activists. This proves once again how strongly Poland is involved in the processes of geopolitical upheaval, especially in Ukraine, and how great Polish efforts are to create and expand their own spheres of interest in Eastern Europe.

The second argument often used by Russia in the past, namely that Ukraine is a "failed state", is not at all suitable to justify a war of aggression

---

[95] https://mronline.org/2023/01/04/on-the-influence-of-neo-nazism-in-ukraine/

that is obviously designed for territorial conquest. It cannot be denied that Russia is not entirely wrong in considering Ukraine a "failed state". Ukraine is by far the most corrupt country on the entire continent. Before the invasion of Russian troops in February 2022, Western media were still clearly critical of Ukraine, especially with regard to existing corruption. The cosmetic repairs currently being carried out by the media-effective replacement of a few ministers do nothing to change the actual problem and are nothing more than whitewashing. As long as this country is headed by a President who has a multi-million dollar fortune and accounts in the Caribbean tax-havens, nothing will change in the overall situation. All the purges and dismissals by this person are merely a show for the media. Russia has clearly shown with its attack on Ukraine that it no longer recognises Ukraine's territorial integrity and state autonomy. Some have even argued that most Russians believe Ukraine is Russia or should still be part of Russia. But why is this so, after Ukraine was internationally recognised as a state and even maintains an embassy in Kiev? After the declaration of independence on 24th August 1991, and the Budapest Memorandum, drawn up in 1994, in which Russia, the United Kingdom and the USA jointly declared to Kazakhstan, Belarus, and Ukraine their willingness to recognise their sovereignty and their borders upon condition that all Russia's nuclear arsenal be given up.

Here is a brief summary of the content of the points:

Article 1:
Reaffirms the commitment of the signatory states to respect sovereignty and existing borders and refers to the Helsinki Final Act as the basis for the principles of sovereignty, inviolability of borders and territorial integrity.

Article2:

Reaffirms the duty to abstain from violence and refers to the Charter of the United Nations as the basis for the prohibition of violence.

Article3:

Reaffirms, with further reference to the Helsinki Final Act, the obligation to refrain from economic coercion aimed at subordinating the exercise of inherent sovereign rights by Ukraine to its own interests and thus securing advantages of any kind.

Article 4:

Reaffirms the commitment to immediately engage the UN Security Council in support of Ukraine if it is threatened with nuclear weapons as a non-nuclear weapon state and a participant in the Nuclear Non-Proliferation Treaty.

Article 5:

Reaffirms the commitment to abstain from the use of nuclear weapons against non-nuclear weapon states that are participants in the Nuclear Non-Proliferation Treaty.

Article 6:

Contains a pledge to consult in the event of conflict.

The fact is that this is a Memorandum, not a treaty, and so is only a declaration of intent under international law and is not itself legally binding. This is the argument of both Russia and the USA, depending on who is accusing whom of what. Russia also argues that this memorandum was never ratified by the Russian State Duma and therefore only represents a declaration of intent by Boris Yeltsin's administration. Was that it then with Ukraine's sovereignty? Not quite! In 1997, Russia concluded the Russian-Ukrainian Friendship Treaty with Ukraine.[96] In this treaty, Russia again assured Ukraine of territorial integrity and inviolability of borders (being the old Soviet Socialist Republic administrative borders). The treaty entered into force in February 1999, after ratification by the Russian State Duma, for an initial period of ten years. The treaty automatically renewed for a further ten years unless a party gave at least six months' notice that it did not wish to renew. There was a clause in this treaty that stipulated that both parties to the treaty undertook not to join any alliance that would be directed, in any way whatsoever, against the other party to the treaty. It is rationally and logically incomprehensible why the West, in the knowledge of these facts, nevertheless implemented an eastward expansion of NATO in 1999 and 2004 and then topped it all off in 2008 with the announcement that it wanted to admit Georgia and Ukraine into NATO. Especially since it must have been clear at that time that the Russian Federation would never accept that Crimea, with its strategically prominent Black Sea ports and the naval base of Sevastopol, would fall into the sphere of influence of Western alliances led by the USA. This move virtually suggests that a provocation of Russia was intended to bring about a confrontation. Especially since the Ukrainians explicitly excluded this involvement in their friendship treaty. The announcement by Ukraine after the Orange Revolution in 2004 that it would reorientate itself towards the West and seek membership in both the EU and NATO, and the subsequent approval of this by both institutions with the start of corresponding accession talks, was, in view of the existing friendship treaty, an unmistakable announcement that it would sooner or later breach the treaty or allow it to expire at a certain point in time.

---

[96] https://en.wikipedia.org/wiki/Russian%E2%80%93Ukrainian_Friendship_Treaty

The action taken by Ukraine up to that point could already be interpreted as a breach of the Russian-Ukrainian friendship treaty. In addition
to this treaty, another treaty was concluded with Russia in 2003, referring
to the 1997 Friendship Treaty, which realigned the course of part of the
border between Russia and Ukraine. This was the Russian-Ukrainian border treaty. Whether this border treaty with Ukraine, concluded in 2003,
became obsolete when the friendship treaty expired, and whether this
treaty was ratified, could not be clarified at the time of going to press.
Based on the facts presented and the fact that since Ukraine's declaration
of independence there has been a clear trend of the population in Crimea
moving towards Russia, the annexation of Crimea in 2014 is far more
complex in its consideration than it is willingly presented by the compliant
Western mainstream media. We will leave out the most frequently presented argument of the donation of Crimea by Nikita Khrushchev, as many
will be familiar with it. That such things occurring within the old Soviet
Union were meaningless as long as Moscow had complete control, goes
without saying. However, there are other interesting aspects to be considered in the overall analysis. Especially in the first half of the 1990s, there
were strong efforts by the so-called Autonomous Republic of Crimea to
endow itself with greater sovereignty. Several attempts in this direction
were stopped by pressure from the Ukrainian government.

The population of Crimea clearly expressed its pro-Russian side in the
elections of 2004 and again in 2010, with Viktor Yanukovych winning the
elections both times with more than an absolute majority. The plan of the
then elected pro-Western President Viktor Yushchenko, who announced
on 4th May 2005 that he would replace the staff of all local administrative
authorities in Crimea, did not lead to the desired result either. The referen-

dum held by secret ballot by the same Crimean Government elected while still in Ukraine, on 27th February 2014, was not recognised by the UN, doubtless because of USA influence, produced a result similar to that of the presidential election. The UN also invokes the primacy of the principle of territorial integrity of all member states enshrined in the UN Charter, the Budapest Memorandum of 1994 and the Ukrainian-Russian Friendship Treaty of 1997 in its Resolution 68/262 adopted in the General Assembly. However, UN General Assembly resolutions are not binding under international law. International law is to a large extent open to interpretation and can be, or is often, interpreted differently. Therefore, the question of which treaties are legally binding turns out to be the most important one.

Equally, significant seems to be the question of where the people of Crimea want to belong, because the right of self-determination of peoples or parts of the population within states has a weight that should not be underestimated, but is regularly subordinated under international law to the constitutions of states, which usually exclude secession. This is a dilemma familiar to the Catalans1 2 or the Basques in Spain, which the Scots themselves recently disagreed on and which continues to trouble South Tyrol.

But in Ukraine, too, there have been attacks and discrimination as well as oppression of the majority Russian population in eastern Ukraine in recent years, before the minor invasion of Russian troops in 2014. This may not be the case in Crimea prior to the disputed referendum, but the fact that the majority Russian population there differs from the majority in Ukraine, especially as Ukrainians strongly emphasise their own identity as being different to Russians – reinforced by massive nationalist and anti-

Russian rhetoric. As one can see, such questions of international law are not as clear-cut or easy to deal with as is often the case in the leading media or through statements by so-called experts and politicians. The media also like to refer to the "NATO-Russia Founding Act" when it comes to explaining "transgressions" on the Russian side. But this is not particularly helpful either, since under international law, as in the case of the Budapest Memorandum, it is only a declaration of intent and not a ratified legally binding treaty. Even the US-Americans, who like to refer to the Memorandum when they think the Russians have done something wrong, once made this clear through their embassy in Minsk.[97] It was officially announced by the USA that the Memorandum was classified as not legally binding.

Whether the aforementioned border treaty of 2003 has legal force or not is becoming one of the central questions to be clarified. Was it ratified independently of the friendship treaty, and does the latter still exist independently of it? Should this be the case, the Russians would no longer be able to talk their way out of having committed a breach of treaty on the one hand and also violated the UN Charter by waging a prohibited war of aggression against Ukraine on the other. This also applies in the event that Ukraine was the first to break the friendship treaty through its NATO accession aspirations. If the aforementioned border treaty was not ratified, there is theoretically no other legally binding and still legally valid treaty regulating the course of the border between Russia and Ukraine. Be that as it may, a clean solution must be found for the benefit of the civilian population. However, this can only be found at the negotiating table and with the involvement of the people on the ground and through neutral mediators.

---

[97] http://minsk.usembassy.gov/budapest_memorandum.html

A question that is often discussed in the media, but also among the population, is whether Germany, or generally a state that supplies weapons to Ukraine, itself becomes a party to the war. There are widely differing opinions on this. First, there is the fundamental view that, according to international law, the delivery of weapons is considered a violation of the right of neutrality. This requires equal treatment of combatants, and it also prohibits the supply of weapons, ammunition, and other war material, as well as support through the provision of militarily relevant information. (In June 1915 the Austro-Hungarian Minister for Foreign Affairs formally complained to the USA Ambassador in Vienna regarding traffic in munitions etc., by the USA to Great Britain as a violation of the accepted rules of war.) Violations of these obligations can be punished by a warring party with countermeasures up to and including the use of military force. This is what international law provides for. But this is only the beginning of the analysis. In the system of collective security of the United Nations Charter, the use of force was prohibited in principle. In the event that the aggressor could be precisely identified, the Security Council was empowered to adopt measures necessary to restore peace. However, this procedure only works if the potential aggressor is not one of the five veto powers that can prevent the adoption of a corresponding resolution. Russia is one of these veto powers and, of course, did exactly that and in this case the previously mentioned right of neutrality had to apply again.

There are also voices that argue that the arms deliveries can be justified by the collective right to self-defence according to Art. 51 UN Charter.[98] This right enables a state, in the event of an armed attack on another state, to support the attacked state by all means, apart from participating in the

---

[98] https://unric.org/de/charta/#kapitel6

fighting with its own armed forces. However, according to the second sentence of Article 51 of the UN Charter, this also requires that these measures be reported immediately to the Security Council. The Federal Republic of Germany did not do this, as Germany would automatically have become a party at war with Russia (co-belligerent[99]). In international law, however, wars are generally considered illegal and the law of neutrality does not apply. Based on the Briand-Kellogg Pact, which became part of international law, war as a means of resolving international disputes is to be outlawed in principle. It legitimises supporting the attacked state with weapons. The obligation of neutrality towards the aggressor no longer applies. The term "non-warfare" takes the place of neutrality. The use of a different term was intended to show a clear distinction from the original concept of neutrality, in order to set out the legal position of parties who oppose the aggressor without themselves becoming a party to the war. Like so much in international law, this statement of the facts is not entirely uncontroversial. Due to Russia's veto in the UN Security Council, a special emergency session of the General Assembly was convened at the Council's request. Here, no member has a veto. After the special session, the General Assembly adopted a resolution on 1st March 2022 demanding an immediate withdrawal of Russian troops from the territory of Ukraine. We recall, according to international law, the clear identification of the aggressor precludes the application of the law of neutrality with the duty of impartiality. Non-application of the law of neutrality has no effect on states not involved in the war. Relations between non-belligerent and belligerent states are still governed by the law of peace, which leaves states free to supply arms and other war material within the limits of their general freedom of action. So much for international law.

---

[99] Co-belligerent is the waging of war in cooperation against a common enemy with or without a formal treaty of military alliance.

Based on this, there are people who are of the opinion that supplying arms to an apparently illegally attacked state is the least that Germany or other states should do. Apart from the fact that one can seldom fight fire with fire and that a German position as a neutral broker could presumably have contributed to the cessation of hostilities, there is also the question of to what extent the Federal Republic of Germany should go so far out on a limb vis-à-vis Russia and thus also take sides unilaterally with Ukraine. In Russia, papers and interviews are circulating which clearly deny the sovereignty of Germany and the Federal Republic of Germany. On the following pages, we will try to discuss whether and to what extent there is any truth in these assumptions.

Since 15th March 1991, according to official records, we have eliminated the post-war order in Germany with final validity. Accordingly, Germany is sovereign in internal and external affairs. If, on the other hand, one looks at the behaviour of the German government in the case of the attack on the two Nord Stream pipelines, one has to raise justified doubts about its actual sovereignty. The German government did not even itself consider this act of terrorism, which according to international law is an act of war if carried out by a state actor, as an attack on Germany, as it involved attacks on essential infrastructure facilities. As we all know, hardly anyone in Europe – neither from politics nor the media – had shown the courage to clearly demand an explanation, to intensively research, question and name the main suspects. In Germany, Sahra Wagenknecht of the party "Die LINKE" and the party "Alternative für Deutschland" were the notable exceptions. By all serious indications, it is the USA, alone or at least in the lead, that carried out this act of state terror against European energy infrastructure. According to the publications of Seymour Hersh, this suspicion, which was already publicly expressed by the author[100] immediately after the attack, has been strongly consolidated. According to Hersh, the USA had carried out an act of war against Germany.

US President Biden even publicly announced his intention to do something "about" Nord Stream, and Chancellor Scholz himself was present at this press conference and showed no reaction. This is an open declaration of bankruptcy by the German government and, in the author's opinion, it borders on treason on the part of the German government to have remained inactive here. There is now even evidence to suggest that the Chancellor was plausibly complicit.[101] The latest publications of Western mainstream press on the blasts could hardly be more ridiculous. The CIA and BND have allegedly found out that a group of Ukrainians and Poles carried out this attack. They chartered a sailing boat and allegedly used it to transport about 400-500 kg of synthetic explosives in addition to the necessary diving equipment. As one can easily research on the internet, diving at these depths is extremely complicated and risky. According to the research, the investigators were able to detect traces of explosives on the table in the cabin. In Germany, the Attorney-General declined to comment. A spokesperson for the federal government only referred to the ongoing investigation by the Federal Prosecutor General. In the context of all that is known, the establishment of a "Nord Stream 1 & 2" committee of enquiry in the Bundestag, Germany's highest parliament, is no longer an option, but mandatory, and this motion must be brought to parliament by the opposition.

---

[100] https://www.youtube.com/watch?v=iBFTHk5zUbc
[101] https://www.tichyseinblick.de/kolumnen/aus-aller-welt/seymour-hersh-nordstream-2-scholz/

There are three parties in the opposition in the German Bundestag. Now, one would assume that the largest party in terms of seats, as the leader of the opposition, would take the initiative and demand or request such a committee of enquiry. However, this is not the case: the CDU Party has so far seen no reason to do so. Neither has the Die LINKE Party, from whom one would have expected it, given their affinity with Russia. It was the "Alternative for Germany" that introduced a motion to set up a committee of inquiry[102] in the Bundestag on 15th March 2023. Up to the time of going to press (6th June 2023), it was not clear whether such a committee of enquiry would be set up or not. Considering the usual way in which the other parties have dealt with AfD democratic motions over the past years, which have all been categorically rejected regardless of the quality of the content, the prospects for a committee of enquiry are not particularly good. It is a particularly interesting phenomenon of these parties, which claim to be democratic in their convictions and thus always propagate tolerance towards dissenters, but in the case of the "Alternative for Germany", whose politics are clearly in the traditional conservative camp, one regularly loses sight of this democratic claim. If one observes the behaviour of the German government more closely, it is no wonder that some people doubt the state sovereignty of the Federal Republic of Germany for a variety of reasons and voices are raised regarding the lack of a peace treaty. Even in Russia, these discussions have already been held in the public media. One could get the impression that such discussions mainly serve to distract from the actually important, mostly topical issues that have a significant impact on society or the immediate development of the country. Since this topic is already being discussed internationally, and it also has a

---

[102] https://www.bundestag.de/dokumente/textarchiv/2023/kw11-de-untersuchungsausschuss-nordstream-936464 ; https://dserver.bundestag.de/btd/20/059/2005989.pdf

certain geopolitical relevance in terms of how one should assess the Federal Republic as a state, we will briefly examine the essential aspects.

The official view is that with the 2+4 Treaty, all post-war matters concerning Germany as a whole should be concluded. For this reason, a formal peace treaty for WWII was no longer necessary. According to Foreign Minister Genscher, this was also intended to avoid further possible claims for reparations. However, the legitimate question now arises: If full sovereignty has been restored, both internally and externally, why are some points of the 1955 Transitional Agreement still in force, and what is the meaning of the term "fossilised occupation law"? This is occupation law, which was already not subject to any disposition by the German state authorities at the time of the conclusion of the Transitional Treaty. The legal view is that the Federal Republic of Germany voluntarily entered into a commitment under international law, and that this is evidence of the outflow of its sovereignty.[103] In this context, however, it is not logically comprehensible for what reason one voluntarily submits, to permanent occupation law, which, among other things, prevents violations of human and international law by the former Allied wartime enemies from being punished, since the aggrieved parties continue to be denied the right of action due to the continued existence of part of the Transitional Treaty. In view of the principle of equality, ius respicit aequitatem, (The law respects equality) which is not only anchored in German law but in almost every democratic legal system and at the same time represents the supreme principle of the ‚Universal Declaration of Human Rights'[104], the aforementioned restriction violates it.

---

[103] Deutscher Bundestag WD2-108/06

[104] Article 1. All human beings are born free and equal in dignity and rights. They are endowed with reason and conscience and should act towards one another in a spirit of brotherhood.

It is extremely regrettable that it is seldom possible to discuss or publish such and similar issues in a civilised manner in Germany without being subjected to polemical attacks. If one raises such questions, which follow a purely state and international law interest, one is almost reflexively accused of nationalism, extremism, or revisionism and branded as a conspiracy theorist or even as a citizen of the Reich. Such practices are unworthy of a liberal democracy and trample on fundamental rights. They show that the basic understanding of democracy, freedom, research, exchange of knowledge and free expression of opinion is not present in people who react in this way to legitimate questions. Yet these people who want to see such exchange suppressed proclaim for themselves to be the defenders of the free democratic basic order.

Another aspect that is often brought up in connection with the lack of sovereignty is the continued existence of the Enemy State Clause in the UN Charter. The Enemy State Clause is a term that refers to Article 107 and parts of Article 53 of the United Nations Organisation (UN) Charter. Both are exceptions to the general prohibition on the use of force against countries that were part of the Axis powers. This designation was used during the Second World War to refer to all states allied with the German Reich. According to Article 107 of the UN-Charter, as a result of the Second World War, states may take coercive measures against "any state which was during it an enemy of a signatory to the present Charter", while according to Article 53 of the UN-Charter, regional agreements directed against the resumption of an aggressive policy by a former enemy state do not have to obtain the approval of the Security Council before taking measures to prevent further aggression. Even though several agreements have been signed prohibiting aggressive acts against the Federal Republic of Germany and obliging it to adhere to the principles contained in Article

2 of the UN Charter, the Enemy State Clause is still an official part of the UN-Charter.

In 2004, a report by the High Level Panel on Threats, Challenges and Change, appointed by UN Secretary-General Kofi Annan, proposed the deletion of this clause. It was felt that this clause was outdated. On 21st March 2005, the Secretary General recommended the deletion of the clause. However, this can only be done at a General Assembly. At the following 60th General Assembly, from 14th to 16th September 2005, the final document called for the deletion of the Enemy States Clause. To date, however, the deletion of the clause has not been implemented. Since then, 18 years have passed. This data was compiled by the author from a work of the esteemed Scientific Service of the German Bundestag. Unfortunately, it seems to have escaped the attention of the ladies and gentlemen in their research that such a decision to delete the Enemy State Clause was taken as early as 1995, and that Japan applied for the deletion in 1992 out of self-interest. The decision was taken with almost unanimous approval in the General Assembly: 155 votes in favour, none against and three abstentions (Cuba, North Korea and Libya). The Enemy States Clauses, as we have just read, are part of the Charter today, unchanged. The revision of the UN Charter, which is part of international law, requires a two-thirds majority in the General Assembly and, in addition, ratification by two-thirds of the UN members, including all five permanent members of the Security Council. There is no information on whether the ratification process has already been carried out. At the very least, the fact that the clause remains unchanged in the UN Charter speaks against it. It is possible that the necessary majority was not reached in a vote. One is in the realm of speculation here, which could be clarified by a small question put to the German government by a parliamentarian of the German Bundestag.

What remains is the realisation that agreements under international law do not protect against reprisals in this day and age, as we have already seen in the case of the Budapest Memorandum and the NATO-Russia-Act. It therefore remains to be seen whether Russia will take direct measures against Germany, what these might look like, and how they will be justified if the case arises.

In this context, it would be an interesting question what would happen if Germany were to declare the attack on the Nord Stream pipelines as an act of war against itself before the UN Security Council, demand clarification and subsequent action against the perpetrator. Germany had not done this by May 2023. No justification was provided as to why this had not been done so far. Russia, on the other hand, had demanded an official UN Security Council investigation in mid-February 2023.

Ukraine - Where do we go from here? Possible scenarios!

The further course of events is of course very much dependent on what decisions are taken on both sides in the near future. At present, the least likely scenario seems to be that both parties agree on a ceasefire in the short term in order to give the maltreated civilian population some breathing space and to negotiate on possibilities for a peaceful settlement of the conflict through compromise. Unfortunately, neither side is currently willing to do this. It is much more likely that the armed conflict will drag on indefinitely. The supply of weapons from the West is a controversial issue throughout Europe. There are supporters who believe that these deliveries will enable Ukraine to prevail against Russia. There is the expectation of a Ukrainian victory over Russia with the reconquest of territories in the east of Ukraine, including Crimea. Then there are those who fear that this will indefinitely prolong the war without achieving an acceptable outcome for one side or the other, which in turn carries with it the potential for lasting conflict. A possible escalation of the war in Ukraine cannot be ruled out either, due to the massive arms deliveries. The total value of individual licences issued by the German government for the export of military equipment to Ukraine in the period from 1st January 2022 to 12th June 2023 amounts to 7,400,000,000 euros. So, 7.4 billion euros of taxpayers' money spent on providing military support to Ukraine.[105] One can be divided about the delivery of weapons. On the one hand, it is right and important to defend a state under attack against an aggressor who challenges the territorial integrity and sovereignty of the country under attack. On the other hand, what if this aggression is based on provocation? Especially by activities of the attacked country, but also by third states? It remains questionable, despite the amount of weapons that have already been delivered to Ukraine, whether these will have a decisive impact on the final outcome of the war. Here, too, one must be exceedingly critical. Most of those who advocate the continued supply of weapons to Ukraine are apparently unaware of some facts. Russia still has large stocks of all essential materials. Be it tanks, howitzers, ammunition, missiles, aircraft and so on. It therefore remains to be seen what difference the modern battle tanks will actually make on the battlefield.

---

[105] https://www.bundesregierung.de/breg-de/themen/krieg-in-der-ukraine/lieferungen-ukraine-2054514

The widely announced tank offensive, which was in fact forced on the German Defence Minister by Poland and the USA, turned out to be a complete failure after a short period of euphoria. Denmark, the Netherlands, and Finland have withdrawn the delivery of further Leopard 2A6 tanks. Currently, only Germany and Portugal can deliver these modern Leopard tanks from German producers. 14 units came from Germany and 3 from Portugal. Germany, desperate not to be able to deliver even one of the promised two battalions, has now added another four. Poland, which threatened to openly breach the contract if Germany did not give permission to deliver, is also currently facing a serious bottleneck, as their tanks are not operational due to their condition. The condition of the tanks promised from Spain was also unclear until recently. It was not until 22nd April 2023 that it became known through the media that six Leopard 2A4s would be on their way to Ukraine by now and four more would follow, which are currently still being repaired. However, there is no longer any talk of the Leopard 2A6s, which have been upgraded in combat value and remain in Spain for the country's own defence.[106]

It is somewhat tragically ironic that Germany, which was forced to deliver battle tanks and made itself available as coordinator, is now the only country besides Portugal to deliver these modern weapon systems to Ukraine. Perhaps it seems absurd in the present situation, but in the end, when the war escalates and develops in a disastrous direction, others might again claim, "Germany did it; the Germans are to blame!" Indirectly, the USA is already trying to do this similarly, saying that the US only supplied Abraham's M1 tanks because Germany insisted on them and would not have supplied Leopard 2s otherwise. The fact that the USA and Poland

---

[106] https://www.zdf.de/nachrichten/politik/spanien-leopard-panzer-ukraine-krieg-russland-100.html

pushed Germany in this direction seems to have been forgotten already or no longer fits into the new narrative. The most important of all resources in this conflict, however, are the soldiers. Russia can put more than a million soldiers under arms if needed. In the summer of 2022, it was estimated that the Ukrainian army had 500,000 troops. Depending on which sources are used, the losses are sometimes presented as higher on one side, then again on the other. Exact, verified figures are almost impossible to come by in the current situation, where each side is talking up the other side's losses and down its own. Most of the foreign mercenaries left Ukraine after the first three months of the conflict. The reason was mainly great disappointment, as many fighters got the impression that they were being used as cannon fodder by the Ukrainian leadership. The mercenaries were all to fight on the front line after a five-day induction, regardless of their actual abilities. They were supposed to sign a gagging contract that granted them a salary of a mere 225 euros per month.[107] The mercenaries were also contractually forbidden to leave the country until the end of the war.[108] [109] Some people were sent to the front without weapons or with a maximum of 10 rounds of ammunition. This behaviour cannot be described as humane. This means that Ukraine cannot expect a noticeable influx of new fighters from outside at the moment. How many NATO soldiers will officially take off their national uniforms and sign up for service in Ukraine remains to be seen. This question has already been discussed many times. The war materials that Ukraine receives must also be serviced somehow. This is increasingly becoming Ukraine's Achilles' heel. In 10 months at the latest, but probably much sooner, the point will be

[107] https://www.blick.ch/ausland/230-franken-im-monat-verpflichtung-bis-kriegsende-britischer-soeldner-klagt-ueber-knebelvertraege-der-ukrainer-id17310767.html

[108] https://www.economist.com/1843/2022/03/11/fighters-with-ukraines-foreign-legion-are-being-asked-to-sign-indefinite-contracts-some-have-refused

[109] https://exxpress.at/krieg-in-der-ukraine-soeldner-sollen-fuer-225-euro-im-monat-toeten-und-sterben/

reached that these very men will no longer be available in sufficient numbers. This could be a turning point that will possibly decide the future of Europe. Will Ukraine return to the negotiating table at this point, or will one of the geopolitical actors in the region ensure that this conflict moves to a further stage of escalation? Will Lithuania perhaps, in suicidal sacrifice for the salvation of Ukraine as well as the geopolitical concerns of the USA and Poland, let its troops led by example and send them to Ukraine, as has already been suggested by former Lithuanian President Vytautas Landsbergis. Is it Poland that will pose as Ukraine's saviour and occupy the west of the country (Galicia) under the guise of a "peacekeeping force"? Will there be an incident that will provoke the NATO alliance case? At present, almost all escalation scenarios are conceivable. Much will depend on how the Ukrainian spring offensive goes and how effectively the weapons, especially the Western battle tanks, are used by Ukraine. The Russians could try to fortify the over 1610 kilometres front line first in order to strengthen their position and thus take the momentum away from the Ukrainian spring offensive. This would buy the time needed for supplies and the arms industry to follow up with an offensive of their own.

In Russia, the reaction to the deliveries of Leopard 2 tanks from Western countries was furious, but also pragmatic. The motto of the Russians in the fight against a Leopard 2A6 is that the fourth Russian T-72 tank will crack the Leopard. Even if this were not the case, the Leopard would then be ripe for repair and thus off the battlefield again for the time being. According to reports, most of the 14 self-propelled howitzers 2000 are also on their way back to Slovakia for repairs. There, they have so far been prevented from crossing the border by the border authorities. The same problems already occurred in December with MARS multiple rocket launchers, which were then diverted to Germany via Poland due to the urgency.

Regardless of whether one agrees to the arms deliveries or not, Slovakia's behaviour is incomprehensible, since in December 2022 it was agreed bilaterally, between Germany and Slovakia, on a maintenance site in the Slovakian town of Michalovce. Now it is suddenly decided to levy customs duties on the imported weapon systems. Large sums of money are demanded, as the country from which the weapons are imported is a non-EU member, and refinement takes place where the systems are repaired. This is a typical example where first an agreement was reached among NATO allies which was supposed to help Ukraine, and suddenly the import of the weapons stopped for a flimsy reason. Comparable to the promise of the delivery of Leopard 2A6 tanks by the Netherlands, Finland, or Spain and the subsequent withdrawal from it. Is this all about money? Do they want to get rich from this situation, or are there other reasons why these transports are blocked? Such an approach does not inspire much confidence in these supposed allies. One can see so clearly how strong the tensions are among themselves as well. Be it Turkey, which has always had a tense relationship with Greece, or Poland, where the governing party regularly incites its people against Germany on its websites almost on a daily basis.

Another point that must be taken into account in the assessment of the next events and for the reasonableness of further arms deliveries is the maintenance of the arms-supplying countries' own defence capability, which is now clearly being called into question not only in Germany. In the United Kingdom, too, experienced military personnel are now questioning their own ability to defend themselves in the event of an attack. Let us briefly look at some figures for Germany. In the case of the self-propelled howitzer 2000, after deduction of the 14 weapon systems delivered to Ukraine, there are still 94 units in the Bundeswehr's inventory. However, only one third of the remaining howitzers are actually operational.

This means that there are currently just 36 of them.[110] The situation is not much better with the Leopard 2 tanks. As of January 2023, the Bundeswehr has 320 units of this weapon. However, this includes a wide range of configurations from 2A4 to 2A7. There are currently only 130 of them ready for deployment.[111] The delivery of 18 2A6 tanks to Ukraine and the tanks currently in Lithuania must be deducted from this total. This leaves Germany with about 100 functional Leopard 2s, distributed across all stages of development. The Münchner Merkur reported at the beginning of March 2023 that there were only 64 Leopard 2 main battle tanks actually operational.[112] On top of all this, there is also a shortage of large-calibre ammunition for the PZH and the Leopard. There were reports that estimated the amount of ammunition available in the event of a conflict at just 2 days. It is incomprehensible that politicians, after a year of war in Ukraine, did not consider it necessary to ramp up production in this case either. The issue of ammunition is currently of utmost importance because Ukraine seems to be running out of it.

Rheinmetall, Germany's largest armaments company, is now looking for new locations throughout Germany, but also in other European countries, for the production of the new Panther main battle tank, as well as for powder and ammunition production. The town of Großenhain in Saxony has apparently been selected as a potential location for this purpose. No further information on this was available at the time of going to press. Among the civilian population, these considerations are definitely viewed

---

[110] https://www.focus.de/politik/deutschland/bericht-ueber-vertrauliches-papier-nur-jede-dritte-panzerhaubitze-2000-der-bundeswehr-ist-einsatzbereit_id_180814125.html
[111] https://www.morgenpost.de/politik/article237421701/deutschland-leopard-panzer-ukraine-lieferungen-druck.html
[112] https://www.merkur.de/politik/verteidigung-leos-leopard-2-panzer-wie-viele-deutschland-bestand-bundeswehr-92121960.html

critically, as there is a perception of becoming a primary target of attack in the event of war. The production of war weapons in Germany and most other European countries is mostly still in peacetime mode. This means that the possibility of continuing arms deliveries is extremely limited. The approximately 100 Leopard 1 tanks that have been announced, which are roughly equal to a Russian T-72 and are even worse armed in comparison, will not give Ukraine a significant advantage over Russia.

So, in the end, it boils down to three central questions:

1. How many combat-ready men can Ukraine muster?

2. How many more weapons systems can the European states provide before they themselves run out of material?

3. When will this situation be reached?

This situation is expected to occur in the late autumn of this year. It is quite impossible that the West can continue to deliver weapons to Ukraine in the same quantity. The USA may be able to continue supplying, but the European states are already reaching their limits. Whether this will be enough to offset or surpass Russia's material and manpower advantage is questionable. It also remains to be seen how China will position itself in the further course of the conflict, and to what extent so-far-neutral Belarus will be involved in Russia's arms production beyond the current level.

In the event of an escalation of the conflict and the involvement of NATO as a warring party, if it has not already been unofficially involved, further developments would be much more problematic. Whether tactical or even strategic nuclear weapons would actually be used in this case is the big question. The danger at least exists. In the less serious case, the warring parties would limit themselves to attacks on military installations, government structures and possibly administrative institutions. This, too, would entail a multitude of consequences. From the collapse of stock exchanges, parts of the economy, civil unrest, the formation of new alliances and spheres of interest to civil wars or the disintegration of international order, many threatening scenarios are within the realm of possibility. What the world and especially Europe might look like after such a catastrophe is highly speculative. In any case, nothing would ever be the same again. An important point in the overall picture, which is rarely discussed but should nevertheless be considered, concerns the question of the actual strength of the NATO alliance in the event of an escalation. We have already seen how volatile some allies are in the commitments they have made and in their behaviour. Whether this would change in the event of an attack on Poland or the Baltic States remains questionable. The fact that each NATO country may themselves determine the measures it implements, up to and including the use of military force, can in such a situation, despite strategic planning and a supreme command, quickly lead to some countries distancing themselves from the commitments they have made, especially in view of the threat of nuclear war. In this case, even a defeat of NATO would be within the realm of possibility if a complete nuclear escalation between the great powers were still ruled out.

One thing is already certain: Ukraine is the biggest loser of this conflict. Convinced to fight for its own freedom, it was unknowingly harnessed to the USA's geopolitical chariot, on which Poland is also currently riding. By every trick in the book, they are being burnt-out for the goals of others, in the true sense of the word. Even if Ukraine could win this war, the price would be astronomical. The loss of life, whether military or civilian, as well as the destruction, is a tragedy. Believing that it is now a free Ukraine, it will, without realising it, move into dependency. EU and NATO membership will then be on the agenda. With membership in the European Union, Ukraine would forfeit most of the freedom it has gained through regulation, paternalism, and war.

Whether Ukraine would take an advantageous path in the medium term by giving up its extensive non-alignment and integrating into the "Western community of values, economy, and alliances" must be doubted. Unmanageable difficulties would arise for Ukraine as well as for the Western organisations. Corruption is Ukraine's best-known major problem since its independence in late 1991. Other Ukrainian shortcomings would also lead to considerable disputes with the EU if the latter were to apply its standards of the rule of law and transparency here, which, despite their own shortcomings, are still higher than those of Ukraine. Special harmony is not to be expected, as has been seen by the east European nations' disputes with them. Apart from that, Ukraine is already a bottomless pit financially due to its sheer size and the war damage, which can hardly be quantified in the meantime, and would cause the EU considerable disharmony in terms of financial distribution. Indeed, whether Ukraine could ever qualify as a member of the EU under current rules seems doubtful.

In the event of Ukraine's integration into NATO, it would be obvious that the USA, and possibly even Poland, would expand their military presence in Ukraine. The establishment of military bases would be logical to underpin the Alliance's obsessional Russophobia. Protection against real or imagined renewed aggression by Russia could easily serve as a justification. The encirclement of the Russian heartland would then be completed on

184

the European side. (In fact, the same kind of post-WW1 encirclement of Germany carried out by France and her allies.) A possibly destabilised Russia could, under certain circumstances, be put on the desired course relatively quickly with pro-Western politicians, similar to what was done in the days of Boris Yeltsin. Mission accomplished! This may be the goal of some Western hardliners. On the other hand, it is already becoming apparent that much more radical forces in Russia are now gaining support, against which the often-maligned President Vladimir Putin appears to be moderate and balancing. Which political forces in Russia will gain momentum as a result of the war in Ukraine and the open East-West conflict remains to be seen. Whatever the outcome of this conflict, Europe will change. New spheres of influence will emerge, and old structures will come under massive pressure.

At present, there is little to suggest that the neo-conservative hawks in the USA will have success on their side in the medium and long term. The New World Order, with the USA as the sole world power, is now receding into the distance in view of the numerous political-diplomatic, economic and not the least military fronts of the USA. The increasing confrontation with China, currently still mainly economic, can quickly completely overwhelm the USA. The petro-dollar is currently losing acceptance and may lose its position completely in the coming years. To counteract this, USA strategists have spared no expense, effort, or conflict in the past decades. This has affected government finances.

The fronts for the success-hungry hawks, who in recent decades have pursued their goals essentially through destabilisation, arms supplies and wars and the exploitation of natural resources, will increase in number and effectiveness around the world. Whether the neocons, who can reliably be accused of ruthlessness and extremism, have miscalculated their geostrategic actions remains to be seen. There are indications that they are increasingly willing to put all their eggs in one basket. In the event of a military success in Ukraine, even with limitations, NATO will be granted another reprieve, as the Alliance will be touted as a guarantor of peace and an example of solidarity. This would not be true, since all nations acted voluntarily and out of their own calculations or special constraints. However, if Ukraine were to be defeated without escalation, NATO as an institution would find itself in a tight spot, as its usefulness would be justifiably questioned and criticism of its intervention and escalation course would grow louder. On this basis, a European defence alliance of some kind could develop, and the European states could possibly emancipate themselves from the USA to a certain extent.

Europe, Geopolitics and the Question of Morality

Propaganda, obfuscation, and the quest for truth

In the last chapter, it is time to look for solutions and ideas on how to positively counteract the current incendiary politics. What approaches are there to solving the problems raised in the book? In the course of writing this book, new developments have constantly been incorporated into the work and have led to regular adjustments and changes. Nevertheless, the last chapter represents the greatest challenge. The self-imposed task was clear: to show what, in the author's view, is important for Europe, what

Europe needs and what it can well do without, or what should be excluded for the good of the continent in the future. Nevertheless, the last chapter of a book dealing with geopolitics did not feel complete.

For all that we now know about geopolitics, one essential question remains unanswered: Does geopolitics have a fundamentally manipulative and interventionist character, and are geopolitics and ethics thus categorically mutually exclusive? It was this idea that this book was intended to address in conclusion. But before we pursue this philosophical question, let us first turn again to our continent and current politics. The decisions taken by the European Union with regard to the war in Ukraine have neither contributed to a de-escalation of the situation, nor have the sanctions been able to persuade Russia to cease its military actions or even to make far-reaching concessions. Ultimately, they have had the opposite effect and, moreover, have hit the economy in Europe, but especially in Germany, hard. The disadvantages of the spiral of sanctions against Russia have a much more detrimental effect on most European countries than on Russia in the medium term. In summary, the EU's activities, which are described as political mistakes, contribute significantly to fuelling the worsening situation in Ukraine.

However, all Western participants in the war in Ukraine currently seem to be unworldly and focused exclusively on escalation. First, it was the USA, Poland and the Baltic states that persuaded Ukraine, or rather the Ukrainian leadership, that it could emerge victorious from this war and even reconquer the eastern territories and Crimea. In any case, the arms deliveries would make a significant contribution to this. Since the beginning of the war, one has constantly had the impression that the Ukrainian leadership is behaving like a hoard of whining children: I want weapons, I

187

want ammunition, I want rocket launchers, I want tanks... planes... Slowly but surely they have received almost all of their toys, albeit not in the desired quantities. Now Germany has also become a warmonger and one of the biggest arms suppliers to Ukraine. Although some European governments, and above all the German government, had initially clearly rejected a delivery in many areas, they are now eagerly sending various defensive and offensive weapons to Ukraine. So now it has also arrived at the categorically rejected delivery of fighter jets. Whether one delivers or agrees to the delivery of former GDR MIG-29 jets is in fact one and the same. The Poles would have delivered the aircraft anyway, since Poland, as we have seen in the case of the Leopard tanks, is not above open breach of contract.

So why dig yourself in deeper and agree to such a delivery? Maybe it's peer pressure within NATO, maybe it's the spinelessness of a German government that has taken to only implementing orders from the US or NATO leadership and adapting, instead of taking its own position that is in the interests of its own country and its people.

Not a single attempt at de-escalation has been made within the last 6 months - neither by Ukraine nor by NATO. Mediation attempts by others have been rejected, for example by China. Admittedly, Russia did not invite to the negotiating table either. But under the known circumstances and the one-sided partisanship displayed by the united West under the leadership of the USA, the Russian side apparently sees no perspective for further negotiations after the attempts at talks in the first half of 2022.

The credibility of NATO and its members has been dealt a further blow with the major Pentagon leak.[113] The interesting thing about this affair is that only for a short time and in a very limited way did the press report on the contents of these leaked documents. The culprit was quickly found, and the leading media's portrayals were only about the betrayal of secrets as such. A 21-year-old National Guardsman is said to have initially published these documents only in a closed online chat group of young people.

More surprising than this story, however, is the fact, that now that the culprit has been found and this poor sod is literally being driven through the village by the media, hardly any further information is available on the contents of the published documents. The majority of the leading media are not fulfilling their duty of research, revelation and clarification sufficiently, which in Germany applies above all to the public media.

Things that had already become public were now discredited by the allegation of manipulation and falsification of the documents. This method is no longer the latest, but it is extremely popular and helpful among the alleged "fact-checkers" when it comes to hastily dismissing contributions to these documents as "fake news". In the context of all this, it also does not seem particularly surprising that the major media companies, NATO spokespersons, the US leadership and the UK simply continue to disseminate the same publications, which have been factually reduced to absurdity by the leaks, as if nothing had happened. The attentive contemporary therefore has no choice but to submit to the arduous task of seeking out the explosive background information himself in the lesser-known

---

[113] In April 2023, two sets of leaked secret documents from the United States Foreign Intelligence Service began circulating on Twitter, Telegram and 4chan.

media and from specialised authors. What has become known so far even confirms the worst circumstance to be assumed, namely the active involvement of NATO personnel in the Ukraine conflict.

Those who still doubted whether the US or the UK would shy away from falsifying evidence or publishing false information, spying on allies or violating written agreements have now been taught better. Although one is actually well informed about the workings of the USA and the UK and has knowledge of how they operate geopolitically, it surprises even the author time and again to find that he is spot on with the assumptions made. Notwithstanding the fact that this last chapter is supposed to be about Europe and the question of ethics in geopolitics, these new developments are of great significance.

The following is an overview of the most important information known so far from the, Pentagon Leaks':

These documents show that there are up to 150 US and NATO soldiers deployed in Ukraine, 50 of them from the UK alone.[114] They also show that, despite the protestations of all Western participants, US military strategists also see NATO's efforts to encircle Russia and the operations of Ukrainian troops as a single campaign. The effort to disguise the military situation in Ukraine is distinctly questionable. The aim is to present the Ukrainian troops and their prospects of military success against Russia's military in a better light and to make the public believe in an imminent breakthrough by the Ukrainian troops. The documents show that the Ukrainian casualties are far higher than the media have reported and that

---

[114] http://www.theguardian.com/uk-news/2023/apr/11/up-to-50-uk-special-forces-present-in-ukraine-this-year-us-leak-suggests

the Russian losses have been deliberately inflated. This was also intended to persuade more young Ukrainian men to volunteer for military service. In this way, public opinion in Europe is simultaneously manipulated into approving military support for Ukraine.

An editorial in the Washington Post on April 3rd 2023 said that a terrible toll would be taken on the Russian aggressors. A "slaughter", according to the assessment of General Mark A. Milley, Chairman of the Joint Chiefs of Staff. It goes on to say that *"most Western analysts remain confident that Ukraine, supplied with large quantities of weapons by the US and its NATO ally, can use them to build a significant offensive capability".*[115]

In early February 2023, the New York Times claimed that Russian military casualties were approaching 200,000 and this was a clear symbol of how badly President Vladimir V. Putin's invasion had gone, American and other Western officials said.[116]

"The Russian military is short of essential goods and supplies," said Colin H. Kahl, the undersecretary of defence. "They are low on artillery. They lack range ammunition, and they compensate by sending offenders in waves to places like Bachmut and Soledar."[117]

These accounts have now all been exposed as propaganda by the publication of the secret documents. The documents show that the US military estimates that the Russian side has suffered 35,000-45,000 casualties. Contrary to public claims by the US and the Western press that Russian ammunition reserves are running low, it seems that it is rather Ukraine

[115] http://www.washingtonpost.com/opinions/2023/04/03/bakhmut-battle-ukraine-resolve/
[116] http://www.nytimes.com/2023/02/02/us/politics/ukraine-russia-casualties.html
[117] https://www.wsws.org/en/articles/2023/04/12/pers-a12.pdf

that is running low on ammunition. This would at least also correlate with the West's intensive efforts to supply Ukraine with ammunition of all kinds as quickly as possible. According to these secret documents, the Russian side is on the verge of gaining air sovereignty over Ukraine.

In an article titled "U.S. doubts Ukrainian counteroffensive will lead to major successes", the Washington Post refers to internal U.S. military assessments that paint a far bleaker picture of the situation for Ukraine.[118] The publications also describe how the US uses relations with its allies to monitor Russia and China. However, these publications were denied by different agencies from several countries. The AP (Asociated Press) reported that US intelligence has seized on claims by Russian agents that they are building a closer relationship with the United Arab Emirates, where key American military facilities are located. The United Arab Emirates rejected the claims, calling them "categorically false".

Egypt, which receives $1.3 billion a year in American military aid, was planning to sell missiles and munitions to Moscow. Egyptian President Abdel Fattah al-Sisi instructed officials in the know to keep production and delivery secret "to avoid problems with the West" Other indiscretions concerned allegations that South Korean leaders were reluctant to supply artillery shells to Ukraine. It was also mentioned that the Israeli spy service Mossad was opposed to Prime Minister Benjamin Netanyahu's proposed overhaul of the judiciary. A senior intelligence official described the leaks to the New York Times as a "nightmare for the Five Eyes" - the US, Britain, Australia, New Zealand and Canada.

---

[118] /www.washingtonpost.com/national-security/2023/04/10/leaked-documents-ukraine-counteroffensive/

These revelations shed a whole new light on things that have already been covered here and also on all the predictions made publicly. It has by no means anything to do with "conspiracy theory" to state that the methods of NATO under the leadership of the USA are disreputable and that the population is massively influenced or even hindered in its formation of opinion by propaganda through misinformation and one-sided representations. The people of the Western countries are at the mercy of the actions of their political leaders and are condemned to finance these actions through their taxes.

It is precisely this behaviour of continuing to supply Ukraine with heavy war equipment, the training of Ukrainian soldiers in NATO countries, the obvious personnel support by NATO personnel in Ukraine, as well as the constant slogans of perseverance, coupled with the cover-up or distortion of the actual situation in the war zone, that will lead to ever more violent reactions on the part of Russia. In this way, the escalation cascade that is building up cannot be broken - on the contrary, it is being deliberately fuelled.

For this reason, the question of what we actually need in Europe is not only justified, it rather suggests itself, since at this point in time, in mid-May 2023, an escalation up to the use of nuclear weapons by Russia in response to NATO's obvious interference in an armed conflict between two non-NATO countries seems increasingly possible. Representatives of the pro-Western position continue to invoke the international law concept of the "non-belligerent party" in view of the extent of support and obvious active interference by the USA, as well as NATO countries. This is not only to legitimise the actions of "the West", but also to reinforce them with new deliveries and declarations. This leads to the only logical conclusion that this is a premeditated action, which is further underlined by the statement of NATO Secretary General Jens Stoltenberg:

"Ukraine has a rightful place in NATO."

And the main focus of the Alliance, of the NATO allies, is now to

"... ensure that Ukraine prevails".

Thus, the deliberate escalation on the part of NATO has been reaffirmed and leaves no doubt vis-à-vis Russia that NATO is not prepared to resolve this conflict at the negotiating table and thus to take Russia's security needs and sensitivities into account in any way. This formulation does not even give the Russians a choice any more. They are virtually forced to do everything they can to bring this conflict to a victorious end or lose face and their integrity themselves. The use of tactical nuclear weapons can possibly only be averted from this position if Russia does not come under massive pressure in the course of this conflict as a result of the arms deliveries and the planned counter-offensive by Ukraine and if its own arms production can exceed the deliveries of the West again. As mentioned before, the number of soldiers available also plays an essential role. According to Stoltenberg, the NATO states have provided and delivered the equivalent of more than 136 billion euros in military aid since the beginning of the war.[119] That Russia's leadership thus perceives NATO as a warring party is at least not surprising.

It is obvious that solutions must be found as quickly as possible. But what might these solutions look like in concrete terms? As is so often the

---

[119] https://de.euronews.com/2023/04/20/nato-stoltenberg-kiew-ukraine-selenskyj

case, opinions are divided on this. One immutable fact, however, is that the window of opportunity to work out solutions for this and other problems is increasingly closing and the danger of escalation is growing. At this point in time, the chances of an early ceasefire or even a long-term easing of the situation are extremely slim. The risk of a further escalation of the conflict, on the other hand, is extremely high in the author's opinion. The current situation is similar to that of the Cuban Missile Crisis[120] in 1962, which represented a dramatic climax of the Cold War. After the Soviet Union stationed more missiles in the GDR and the USA in England, Italy and Turkey in 1958/59, it was agreed with the Cuban leadership to station more than 40,000 Soviet soldiers and large quantities of weapons on Cuba. Among the weapons stationed were nuclear missiles. The USA was thus exposed to an immediate threat 200 km off its coast. A state of affairs that was unacceptable to the USA and could in no way be reconciled with the US Monroe Doctrine, which clearly defined the Western Hemisphere as an exclusively American sphere of interest and, as we know, still does. It is only thanks to the prudence and conscience of a few on both sides that the unthinkable did not occur at that time. The USA did everything it could to persuade the Soviet army to withdraw from Cuba with its nuclear weapons. The compromise finally negotiated between the two sides stipulated that the Soviet army would withdraw from Cuba and in return the USA would have to retrieve its nuclear missiles from Turkey. This allowed both sides to save face and the status quo was restored. If the Soviets had remained intransigent at that time, an escalation to nuclear war would have been highly probable. Today's NATO and US strategists seem to assume that if Ukraine were fully integrated into the West's sphere of influence, they could freely station weapons of all kinds there without the Russian government being able to do anything about it. The desire to

---

[120] https://en.wikipedia.org/wiki/Cuban_Missile_Crisis

present the Russians with a fait accompli with Ukraine's membership in NATO has probably been the father of all further thoughts. This assessment is both naïve and unworldly, and above all it is extremely dangerous. The Chinese will undoubtedly observe the actions of the USA and NATO even more intensively in the future and draw their conclusions in dealing with the USA in the South China Sea. The author dares to doubt whether China will rely on verbal promises from the USA in the future. Regardless of the outcome of this conflict, a fundamental course must be set for Europe that will lead to a long-term improvement of the political and social situation and thus prevent renewed destabilisation. Europe needs a common voice. However, not on just any topic of the socio-political zeitgeist, but on such important issues as defence and peace policy, the economy and trade. Here it is necessary to reach a sustainable consensus at the European level.

The diversity of the European nations should be highlighted and used as an advantage instead of smothering this under a bell of feigned equality and brotherhood. The often preached equality of European nations under the umbrella of the EU is in reality window dressing. This can be seen in the financial inequity in the EU alone, which increasingly raises questions and stirs up ill will and discord among the nations. Last but not least, the euro has led to considerable distortions within the countries of the monetary union. The common currency now represents a ticking time bomb for all member countries involved. The regulatory frenzy of the European Union is diametrically opposed to basic democratic ideas, and so the EU has already effectively declared itself obsolete. The EU in this form has failed due to its manifold presumptions and its own untrustworthiness and obesity. That is why the motto for the future must be less instead of more bureaucracy. More communication at eye level, instead of following instructions from on high in Brussels or Strasbourg with little opportunity for intervention. The basis for communication, independent of the EU, is the Council of Europe, which was founded in 1949 by 10 states and can serve as an institution for understanding without mutual interference. The Council of Europe now has 49 member states.

Bureaucratism in the European Union has taken on such harmful forms that its excesses now hinder or unreasonably delay sensible and meaningful decisions in almost all political areas. Moreover, decisions are being taken, that will do more harm than good for the people and their regions, living thousands of kilometres away from the Brussels/Strasbourg juggernaut. Europe, with its countries, different conditions and circumstances, needs, customs, state economies and budgets, is too diverse to be able to regulate all political fields and social affairs in a centralised manner. The costs incurred by the exorbitantly excessive administrative structures are wasted tax money that the states, especially the donor countries, lack in their own regions to build and expand their infrastructure or to support their social systems.

Politicians of various parties as well as the leading media want the German people to believe that Germany benefits economically from the EU to a disproportionate extent and that the profit for the German economy is disproportionately higher than the contribution;in fact, it is primarily internationally active large corporations that profit, and not only those based in the EU donor countries. These corporations have not paid taxes in Germany for a long time. It is above all the middle class and the shrinking number of average workers who pay with their taxes. They are also the ones who suffer the most from the burden of the flood of rules and regulations. The broad mass of citizens are paying to have the air they breathe

197

taken away from them. In a nutshell, this means: the European Union in its present state must be subjected to a reversal if freedom, diversity, state sovereignty and the rule of law are to endure in Europe.

A return to the European Economic Community would be an essential step towards normalising the difficult economic situation and, above all, easing the political relations between the states and the regulatory burden on the citizens. It would be the right step to unleash European companies and free them from market distortions caused by a subsidy undergrowth, thus also making them more competitive again. In principle, all decisions made by the European Commission in recent years should be put to the test. In particular, the modern trade in indulgences with CO_2 certificates should be ended immediately. Likewise, the senseless destruction of the European car industry - hand-in-hand with institutions in the USA - testifies to the fact that those responsible in Brussels and Strasbourg have completely lost touch with reality and the processes in the economy, or possibly even deliberately abandoned them. Be that as it may, these and many other decisions are proof that this entangled system needs a complete overhaul.

Europe must finally become aware of its own qualities again and stand on its own two feet, economically, militarily and politically. In doing so, it can only be a first step to free itself from the EU's superfluous bureaucratic and financial ballast. The same applies, incidentally, to NATO in its present form.

In both institutions, the costs, financial and immaterial, are clearly disproportionate to the realisable benefits. The wastefulness already mentioned in the European Union continues in the structure of NATO. Each member country pays hundreds of millions of euros annually for a defence alliance controlled by the USA, which primarily represents the geostrategic interests of the USA. None of the member states is apparently courageous enough to point out the limits to this egomaniacal and dangerous behaviour of the USA. Europe therefore needs its own defence alliance in which European security interests take centre stage.

Ways forward for Europe and a European policy of understanding and peace Recent history clearly demonstrates that NATO is not fulfilling its task of defence due to the massive influence of the USA. Moreover, it is all too obvious that the interests of the USA do not coincide with those of European nations. As already shown, the US is fundamentally concerned with maintaining its own power and expanding its own spheres of interest, irrespective of whether allies are being squeezed in the process. In future, non-European powers must no longer be allowed to exert a decisive influence on the security policy, economy and socio-political concerns of Europe and the European states. The call on the USA to finally adhere to its own Monroe Doctrine in the original version of 1823 is long overdue.[121] This has been deliberately reinterpreted and disregarded by the USA since the beginning of the 20th century on its way to becoming a global empire.[122]

Perhaps it is time for the European states to draft a comparable doctrine of their own with regard to the USA and to work specifically on enforcing it. Russia on the contrary must be included in a future European security and defence concept. Therefore, the settlement of the conflict between

---

[121] The Monroe Doctrine of 1823 stated that European countries should stay out of the entire American continent and its affairs, and that the USA in return should undertaketo stay out of Europe.

[122] https://www.deutschlandfunk.de/praesident-roosevelt-ergaenzt-monroe-doktrin-100.html

Russia and Ukraine and its reappraisal at the European level is also of absolute importance. Dealing with the existing reservations between the Russian Federation and its immediate neighbours, the former Soviet republics, is an essential part of a sustainable peace process for Europe. Only European representatives should cooperate and mediate in this process, to the complete exclusion of American institutions, interest groups and US non-governmental organisations.

The interests of the USA do not coincide with those of European nations

Russia is currently the aggressor, having started this war of aggression. But recent months have shown that its military strength in conventional weapons does not pose a serious threat to Europe. Neither could Russia have afforded a broader front, nor could the Russian Federation have provided more military vehicles or equipment. Nevertheless, numerous media and responsible politicians and so called experts have spread the spectre of Russia possibly intending to invade several countries and spread across the European continent like an octopus.

Once again, people's fears have been played with, in order to justify this massive military support for Ukraine and to promote the demonisation of an entire country, including its people and even its artists. International understanding is supposed to be one of the European or Western values, but with regard to Russia, the complete opposite has been done in the past months and this in turn has been justified with "values". Hatred of Russia was deliberately propagated and "cultivated". This behaviour should be a "nogo" for a supposedly open-minded and tolerant society.

In future, the United Kingdom should also orient itself much more towards Europe and not towards the USA, especially in terms of foreign and defence policy. At this point the British lack the economic and military capacity to take on a special position within the European community of states. History has also shown that the decision to rely on the USA unconditionally led to the loss of the British Empire. From Germany's point of view, the United Kingdom is an important strategic partner with whom we have many historical ties. A closer strategic partnership between Germany and the United Kingdom would be of enormous benefit to both states without any doubt and would also have a positive overall effect on Europe. An agreement must be reached among the European nations that will prevent Europe from once again coming under the all-encompassing influence of a great power in the future. There is also no point in exchanging one hegemon for another. An important point for a positive development in the future Europe is to effectively prevent political influence on individual states, which can lead to the destabilisation of the continent and endanger peace in Europe. It is equally important for all nations in Europe to protect themselves against globally operating NGOs. These heavily funded non-governmental organisations, such as foundations, educational institutions, political network organisations or ostensibly charitable institutions, are under the influence of their financiers, whose manipulative interventions can influence social peace, political decisions or power relations within a country for their own benefit.

A stable Europe also includes a stable Germany. In the author's opinion, it is even an essential component. This means that we Germans must first get rid of the current caste of politicians through democratically legitimised mesures. Germany must learn again to formulate its own interests to represent them and to implement them within the framework of a European dialogue. Building on this, we must once again formulate a foreign policy that can represent these interests at a high diplomatic level vis-à-vis the nations of this world. German interests must once again have priority at home. This does not mean, of course, that this should be done at the expense of other states. On the contrary, broad consensus must be the maxim. However, it is only logical that Germany can only be a good partner if it is domestically and economically stable. In the future, Germany's financial policy must also be "Germany first". Germany must return to the kind of policy for which it was once respected and respected in the world. It must once again concentrate on the European continent and, in the style of Otto von Bismarck, orient its foreign policy towards the goal of reviving and cultivating the historically grown ties in Eastern Europe. For Germany, a genuine and serious peace policy should be the measure of all things, which again takes into account the restriction to the commandment laid down in the constitution to limit itself militarily to national defence. This must also be made clear to other countries and allies. The goal of Germany's new foreign policy must be to repair the damage caused by its flawed Eastern European policy and lack of competence. Above all, the guidelines of German policy should no longer be dictated by outside influence. It goes without saying that relations with Western European states must not be neglected.

With regard to the USA, a clearer distinction must be made between partnership and interventionist ambitions. Interference in the internal affairs of Germany but also of other European states must be rejected as unacceptable. Due to the frequent international interventions which have their beginnings in military bases of foreign powers on German territory, a complete withdrawal of all foreign troops still on German territory should take place. This must be demanded emphatically, at least from the German side. Germany must not continue to be the starting point for military interventions, illegal destruction and killing attacks by US drones or intelligence activities. The proportionate costs incurred for these bases should no longer be borne by the German taxpayer in the future and until they are completely withdrawn.

Independent European peace and defence initiatives, decoupled from the USA and gradually detached from NATO, must be brought into being. It is important to note that this should not be done with consideration for US representatives or the objections of transatlantic network organisations, nor with the involvement of EU institutions, as these essentially only follow transatlantic guidelines and recommendations.

After a peace agreement in Ukraine, relations with Russia must be brought as quickly as possible to a level that at least allows for international understanding, and the sanctions against Russia must be lifted as far as possible in favour of mutually beneficial economic relations. This serves to maintain peace and is in the economic interest of the European states and the Russian Federation. Sanctions that achieve no goal whatsoever and only harm the sanctioning party in the process are nonsense, to say the least. Russia is not Putin and vice versa, which means that one must not condemn the people of a country for the actions of their politicians or government. There are already many young politicians in Russia waiting to replace the old ones. However, with its current foreign policy, Europe and "the West" are helping to boost radical, extreme nationalist forces in Russia. This cannot be desirable. Collective liability of Russian citizens, which leads to even artists and sportsmen and sportswomen being excluded or expelled, must not exist as a matter of principle.In the same way, the attack on the Nord Stream pipelines must be fully investigated. Those responsible must be indicted before the International Criminal Court in The Hague and the attack itself must be condemned as an act of war if it was committed by state actors or military units.

With the orientation of German foreign policy towards the continent, peacekeeping in Europe is once again moving into its focus. Peace in Europe also means security for Germany. Only in a secure environment is positive economic and social development possible. Contributing to the settlement of the conflict in Ukraine should therefore also be the most important task of German foreign policy. At present, however, Germany's highest diplomat is completely unsuited for this task. The solution that has yet to be found must in any case be sustainable and secure peace in the region in the long term. The parties involved should be made to understand that this important task can only succeed at the negotiating table. A continuation of this war will inevitably lead to further stages of escalation. The stationing of tactical nuclear weapons in Belarus and the threat to use them if the worst comes to the worst clearly shows that the strategy of military support for Ukraine has in no way contributed to a pacification of the conflict and rather has the opposite effect. Many experts, also in the West, now take this view and even US military personnel are no longer so sure of this strategy.[123] [124] The announcement by Poland to build up the strongest army in Europe by 2025[125] and to seize buildings in Warsaw used by Russia's embassy for years without proper justification also does little to ease tensions. Unfortunately, it is obvious from everything that has be-

[123] https://moderndiplomacy.eu/2023/04/22/ukraine-cant-win-this-war/
[124] https://therealnews.com/scott-ritter-dont-believe-the-hype-ukraine-cant-win-this-war
[125] https://www.politico.eu/article/europe-military-superpower-poland-army/

come known so far that Poland has no interest whatsoever in de-escalation the situation with Russia.[126]

Germany's increased engagement on the continent should also lead to more intensive cooperation with the Baltic states again, with the aim of promoting the expansion of economic relations and advancing a common defence concept at the European level. This is the only way to gradually regain lost trust. The same applies to relations with Hungary, which have been steadily deteriorating for years. The condescending manner of the EU in its dealings with Hungary has also contributed to this. Here, Germany must strive to continuously improve the damage done to bilateral relations by the Merkel and Scholz governments through cooperation based on mutual respect.

A compromise that is acceptable for Ukraine, Russia and the European security and economic structure must be worked out as quickly as possible and discussed at a European peace and security conference. Only in this way will it be possible to restore the urgently needed understanding on essential issues. For Ukraine in particular, a European peace and understanding conference must be set up to negotiate a compromise that is acceptable to Ukraine, Russia and the European security and economic system. This is not an easy task, but it should be recognised that even the most difficult negotiations are better than prolonging the war now raging even one more day. With good will and without the geostrategically motivated interference of non-European forces, the path to this goal can certainly be considered realistic. Such a conference could give rise to a long-term Ukraine mediation and support body, staffed with European advisers

---

[126] https://www.theguardian.com/commentisfree/2022/nov/13/poland-russia-defeat-ukraine-western-europe

from various countries, which would advise Ukraine internally, monitor events and help to mediate externally between Ukraine and Russia, also involving the other neighbouring Eastern European states. The basic idea behind this is derived from the need for all European countries and regions to consider peacemaking and peacekeeping in harmony as the most important common task. Future active support for Ukraine and cooperation in the economic sphere and help in building a political structure that is less vulnerable to corruption would be imperative for the stabilisation of the country. To this end, functioning administrative structures must be established in order to be able to effectively advance reconstruction. This should be a priority goal for all European states, as it is a central component for a sustainable stabilisation of the political situation in Eastern Europe. The urgently needed improvement of economic performance and infrastructure can only build on this. Here, too, Germany would have to show willingness to stand helpfully by Ukraine's side.

A neutral Ukraine, with Switzerland as a model and a non-aggression agreement with the Russian Federation, is without doubt the most sensible of all solutions, which would offer both parties to the conflict lasting security. The objections raised by Russia would be taken into account by Ukraine, as a neutral state, not seeking further membership in NATO and the EU. This would be a rock-solid basis for normalising relations between the two countries step by step. In this context, it could even be negotiated whether Crimea becomes an independent and neutral people's republic in order to take the tension out of the explosive issue of Crimea in particular. In this way, both Russia and Ukraine could independently establish close relations with Crimea. For the areas of Donbass and Luhansk, the temporary deployment of a large contingent of UN blue helmets to secure peace would be considered sensible. The question of the whereabouts of these two provinces arises first of all from Ukraine's constitution. Secession is seemingly ruled out here, as is the case with almost all state constitutions. Nevertheless, Ukraine must also respect the wishes of the people living there. An internationally monitored referendum could produce a meaningful result. Do the people want to belong to Russia or to Ukraine?

A third option would be to merge the two provinces and establish a neutral autonomous republic, governed by its citizens. This would probably be the most sensible solution, as awarding territories to one side or the other could again lead to tensions. In any case, it is important to find a solution that avoids a complete loss of face for all parties involved, both Russia and Ukraine, and takes into account their respective security needs. NATO, the USA and Poland, as the direct beneficiary, must commit themselves, in order to secure peace on the European continent, not to make any further advances towards integrating Ukraine into NATO or any other Western organisation. The dissolution of the Lithuanian-Polish-Ukrainian brigade would be required by the agreed neutrality, as it was created primarily to carry out missions within the framework of NATO. Likewise, the linking of non-NATO and NATO countries in joint combat units is to be described as extremely unfortunate, since mutual support or deployment of any kind can lead to further military confrontations. Furthermore, the aforementioned states, but also Russia should not interfere in any way in the internal affairs of Ukraine or the other, possibly emerging, neutral republics in order to influence the opinion of the population in this way. In return, Russia must make a contractual commitment to finally recognise Ukraine's territorial integrity as the basis for future peaceful coexistence.

In all that has been said here so far about geopolitics and its application, one thing becomes abundantly clear. Over the last one hundred years, major states, such as Britain, the USA, France, Russia, but also Poland and Nazi Germany, to name but a few, have lacked decency and morality in the implementation of their geopolitical goals. The implementation of objectives had priority, no matter how high the risks to the stability of regions or even entire continents. Two world wars were sparked in Europe in the last century due to unscrupulous geopolitics, which ended in Germany being held solely responsible for these tragedies. Historians around the world have absolved Germany of sole blame for the First World War decades later. The geopolitical events of that time prove all too well how much states such as Great Britain, the USA, France, Poland and Russia were partly responsible, not only for the tragedy of the First World War, but also for the Second. Unfortunately, only a few experts and historians around the world dare to address the question of guilt for the Second World War. Dealing with the path to the outbreak of the Second World War and the guilt for it is taboo, especially in Germany. Immediately, one is accused of revisionism, nationalism or sympathy for National Socialism or even hostility towards Jews or something else, no matter how absurd, if one deals with the time and comes to the conclusion that it could be a bit more complicated than simply explaining it with German sole guilt or National Socialism. But it remains obvious, because a sober look at the geopolitical events in Europe at that time makes it abundantly clear that there were further efforts, suspicion, competitive thinking, fomented hatred, influence and deception on the part of various countries and therefore, on closer inspection, more than one culprit can be identified for the escalation to the outbreak of the war, as well as for its course. This statement is in no way intended to diminish the crimes of the National Socialists and the horrors caused by this regime. The author merely wishes to point out that the complexity of geopolitical processes does not allow for simple and straightforward explanations and that not only one party is responsible for an escalation of this magnitude, neither then nor now. The Cuban Missile Crisis, which could have led to a major war, was also preceded by a multi-layered, multi-year history.

This fact now leads to the only logical conclusion: Russia, too, cannot and must not be condemned today as the sole culprit in the current situation, since the overall picture and all the essential facts speak against it. It may seem surprising to some, but even the USA does not bear sole responsibility for the current situation, although it has contributed disproportionately to the current situation with its hegemonic and unscrupulous geopolitics. But there are also always players who ride the wave of the success of other states and their policies. These, let us call them opportunistic-participatory oriented states, also bear a responsibility, especially if they contribute directly or indirectly to a possible escalation of the conflict through their activities.

Much of what is mentioned here is of course pure theory or vision. However, a vision that could well have the potential to be put into practice. Of course, preconditions have to be created for this. Some of the fine-sounding ideas mentioned here require a profound rethinking of the way geopolitics is viewed and applied. Above all, a rethinking is needed with regard to the consideration of states that have hitherto been regarded as allies or partners, their motivations and approaches. The events described in this book inevitably lead one to suspect that geopolitics and morality are largely mutually exclusive. Even without reference to this, one is likely to realise that what has been covered here so far is only the tip of the iceberg.

The abysses opened up by the practice of unconscionable geopolitics can be found worldwide and scattered over millennia of human history.

The prerequisite for moral development in geopolitics is an understanding of the deed and effect or impact triggered by a particular strategy in a geographical space. Since it is in the nature of a state to develop as an entity, the question is therefore not whether, but only when and how geopolitical considerations are made at a given point. The development of the state is an ongoing process that takes place on many social and societal levels. Its development, however, depends largely on the moral compass of the persons in charge. Normally, this development is designed to increase the power and influence or wealth of a state, its rulers, leadership or certain influential groups within the system through outward strategic or warlike considerations and the application of geopolitical measures. The drift from genuine concern for the prosperous people towards an almost pathological need for an unlimited accumulation of power and influence or wealth usually leads, in history as in the present, to the loss of morality and decency in foreign policy. Applied geopolitics and ethics have so far mostly been irreconcilable. In groups, it is inevitable that different views and opinions or sensitivities clash. This leads to an increased risk of conflict, which is caused by different levels of moral development and mindset of the individuals involved. The likelihood of violent confrontations between the groups increases exponentially. Of course, it is also possible that different views within the groups will lead to disputes and corresponding divisions. This danger is greatly increased by scheming individuals who, by launching lies and allegations or indiscretions, can create mistrust, rejection, hostility and strife among themselves even in a small group. A community can thus be destroyed quickly and effectively. Individual members fall by the wayside, disappointed and demoralised. The only thing that can help against this is a frequent open exchange that analyses the causes of disputes at an early stage. This is the only way to prevent destructive confrontation and identify troublemakers. What works in small groups also works on a large scale and can also be transferred to states. The targeted identification and filtering out of egomaniacs, duplicitous players and provocateurs would be an important step in preventing misunderstandings and defusing impending conflict potential at an early stage. For this purpose, a discussion format on a multilateral level would be recommended, in which high-ranking diplomatic representatives exchange views in regularly recurring meetings. At this level, misunderstandings could be cleared up and the sensitivities and interests of the parties involved could be openly discussed in order to find compromises and solutions together. At this level, lobbyists, representatives from business, finance and geostrategic network organisations would be excluded. For this, it is also crucial that, by defining a clearly and unambiguously formulated "modus operandi" with regard to the deliberations and application of geopolitical measures, one commits oneself not to unscrupulously carry out one's interests on the backs of other, mostly weaker states. One could also call the whole thing the rules of the game for the grand chessboard.[127] Mutual respect is one of the basic conditions for good and stable international relations. At least that is how it should be. If this is not present, sooner or later this leads to a point where destructive geopolitics becomes the accepted means.

---

[127] The Grand Chessboard: American Primacy and Its Geostrategic Imperatives, 1997

Clear signs of geopolitics without morals and scruples are:

• Intervention by infiltrating political organisations and influencing decision-makers.

• Bribery, formation and financing of opposition groups or parties.

• Fomenting civil war and coups

• Assassinations of politicians or media representatives.

• The falsification of alleged evidence.

• Destroying economic foundations and entire state budgets.

• Waging wars and proxy wars.

These methods are unfortunately part of the standard repertoire of some actors and have been for a hundred years and more.

One could counter the demand for a moral basis by arguing that such restrictions would make it impossible to effectively enforce state interests and that other, competing states might even interpret this as weakness. The justifications for disregarding such ethical and moral principles in geopolitics could be extensive. But all these objections are based on the hypothetical assumption that ethical principles could not be registered, honoured and applied equally by other states and governments.

The strongest and most ruthless actor can afford to act without any ethical consideration, but in the long run it will only leave scorched earth. As a result, others who have been victims of this behaviour may form new alliances and strategic partnerships. If one pays some attention to the Chinese way, one realises that China's international and geostrategic approach is different. Here, the focus has so far been exclusively on contracts, investments and gigantic infrastructure projects. To a certain extent, this is an economic geopolitics. In the meantime, this has taken on gigantic proportions and, measured against this, is proceeding almost silently. Some projects are reported in the Western media from time to time, such as the New Silk Road, the purchase of port facilities or industrial sites and companies in key industries. What is not heard in connection with this are wars, unrest, coups or direct military interventions by China - at least not so far! The open Chinese claim to Taiwan can develop into a full-blown conflict relatively quickly, especially because US interests collide with China's here. Apart from that, there is currently no evidence of Chinese interference in the affairs of other states. Meanwhile, China is aware of its military strength and the USA can no longer act in the old Wild West manner towards China. The global organisation of the BRICS states, in which China as well as Russia, India, Brazil and South Africa have joined together to form a powerful economic and financial alliance, shows how geopolitics and world power politics can be pursued without military interventions and the destabilisation of entire states and regions. Consequently, cooperation at eye level and a transparent foreign policy in which interests are openly formulated and negotiated is not something that common sense negates, but at most something, that could be rejected by sick egomaniacs, megalomaniac hegemons or imperialists. For this reason, it is high time to initiate a paradigm shift in Western geopolitics.

213

The maxim of a new geopolitics should be:

"The sovereignty of a state, its integrity and the integrity of the nation are the basis and yardstick for the application of modern geopolitics, the foundations of which are ethics and morality, which are also an obligation. It is equally obligatory not to assert one's own political interests against the will and at the expense of the integrity of another nation. The guideline for this must be an ethical and moral compass created by the community of nations"

Although there are only a few states in this world that have the capacity to engage in offensive and aggressive geopolitics and thus manipulatively influence the development of another state, a commitment to refrain from such action should nevertheless have universal validity and be accepted equally by all states. A state's commitment to refrain from such action could even serve as a seal of approval for its own foreign policy in a certain sense. For this purpose, framework conditions must be created at the international level. A commitment of states within the framework of the United Nations and the integration of certain procedural rules into the UN Charter would be a possible way to anchor this code of conduct in international law in a universally valid way. The highest principle must be to refrain from interfering in the internal affairs of other states. No attempts may be made to infiltrate governments, to blackmail or to engage in activities that influence, destabilise or change the political system of a state and the formation of opinion to the advantage of the other. Interference in the internal affairs of a state by third parties must in future be considered a violation of international law. Violations of this future set of rules should certainly result in severe penalties. In all the good intentions, however, one must by no means forget the non-state actors. The so-called non-governmental organisations (NGOs) that, without attracting much attention, also cause governments to fall and regions of the world to be shaken by unrest. Since most of these are foundations that are subject to national law, the states must integrate appropriate safeguards into national foundation law. Hungary, for example, which has successfully resisted interventions by George Soros' Open Society Foundation, can serve as an example.

In this way, the current gap between ethics and geopolitics could be permanently eliminated and made all-encompassing, since in this way it can no longer be misused as a highly manipulative instrument in foreign, security and economic policy. This would not only secure peace in Europe and beyond, but also ensure a noticeable reduction in the potential for international conflict worldwide.Despite all the hypothetical considerations, the immutable fact remains that the real responsibility lies, as always, with the people, i.e. the decision-makers in politics. Some of them are responsible for the deaths of innocent people and indescribable destruction in unnecessary wars. Some of them may not even be aware of this, because they lack knowledge of the connections and do not notice how they themselves are manipulated and used. It is indeed disconcerting to see how politicians of our time repeatedly try to fight fire with fire and assume that the next time they will achieve a different result than before. So it remains unfathomable to common sense what such erroneous assumptions are based on and why the broad mass of humanity demonstratively displays the appearance of obtuseness. The only thing that remains for the alert observer is the wish that a paradigm shift will take place here as well.

New thinking usually emerges with the advent of a new generation that does not make the mistake of blindly following in the footsteps of its predecessors. The hope for change thus rests on the shoulders of the coming generation of young people who feel called to shape politics in the future. This generation also has the desire for a future worth living, which may only be accessible if one is prepared to break new ground in politics. It is those among the young who go through life with their eyes open, who value education and free thinking, who form their own opinions objectively and based on facts, and who thus take on the task of initiating a change in politics and the economy in the near future. Above all, the ethics of action must also be established in international strategies. The hope that the majority of those currently in charge will engage in this process of rethinking is more than questionable, since they have already become too accustomed to the supposedly comfortable feeling of power and wealth and have voluntarily subordinated themselves to the existing system. Nevertheless, an appeal to those who are responsible for the many miseries cannot hurt.

Due to his political work, the author has been able to establish many contacts in Germany and other European countries, which in some cases have developed from purely political work into friendships. Thus, it can be said with certainty that from Estonia to Serbia and from Italy to Norway, there are people who have the fate of their country and that of Europe at heart. It is to all of them that this book is dedicated, marking the beginning of a work that should contribute to stimulating the process of a geopolitical paradigm shift. This idea is accompanied by the hope that the moral foundation of these people is firmly rooted and that they will be able to resist the temptations of money and power, and that instead ideals and ethical foundations will increasingly become the driving forces behind their work in the future. Europe is not just a concept. It is our homeland and the source of our identity. It stands for our traditions and values, which have developed over generations. We Europeans must not be allowed to let this be taken away from us by influential lobby groups, their organisations and politicians influenced or even installed by them. Europe is more than the sum of its parts, and Europe is not the EU. What the EU calls Europe today in its supposed glory does not come close to what Europe actually is for the peoples of this continent. Europe must once again become a place full of inspiration and innovation. It needs to redefine itself as European again and shake off colonial guilt complexes and imposed egalitarianism. What the European Union cannot achieve, a community of sovereign states in Europe, built on equality and trust, can create. However, this necessary innovative force of Europe can only be ignited if it is not subject to a constant influence from outside, which is preoccupied with sustainably thwarting the enormous potential of this continent or exploiting it for its own interests. The longing for peace unites the European peoples on a fundamental level. At the same time, it is also the differences that lead to synergy effects and thus bring people closer together. We Europeans should love our nations and honour their traditions, but never lose sight of the fact that our countries are all parts of a great whole that we must cherish and protect: EUROPE!

Photo credits:

P. 23: Friedrich Ratzel, Source: Wikipedia/OS

P. 23: Rudolf Kjellen, , Source: Wikipedia/OS

P. 24: Karl Haushofer, Source: Wikipedia/OS

P. 27: Zbigniew Brzeziński, License: CC BY 3.0 de, Terms of use: Creative Commons Attribution 3.0 de Created: 2014-02-01 20:16:03

P. 40: Otto Fürst von Bismarck, Source: Wikipedia/OS

P. 59: "No fly zone Lybia" Autor: Jolly Janner CC01 PD

P. 60: Hillary Clinton Source: Screenshot YT

P. 82:Swiss Institue for peace and energy, Autor: Alexandre Beaurieux

P. 85: Sir John Halford Mackinder, Source: Wikipedia/OS

P. 86: Heartland Theorie Quelle: Source: Wikipedia/OS

P. 87: Nicholas J. Spykman, Source: Wikipedia/OS

P. 105 Screenshot YT abc-news "Under fire in Ukraine" 2014

P. 105/106: Screenshots YT "Kharkiv_UA Title: 'Революція Україна Київ закріплення позицій на вул.Грушевського 22.01.2014р.'"

P.124 Caricature Poland/Lithuania 1930s Source: Wikipedia /OS

P.126 Map, Intermarium, Source Wikipedia /OS

P.129 Extract from the minutes of the Potsdam Conference. Source:

P.146 George Soros, Source: Wikipedia / OS

P.200 Caricature of the Monroe Doctrine 1930s. Source: Wikipedia / OS

OS: Open Source, PD: Public Domain, YT: Youtube

Related Link Collection

Europe:

https://www.gmx.net/magazine/politik/grieche-nervoes-erdogan-droht-athen-raketenangriff-37553128

https://greekcitytimes.com/2023/01/16/erdogan-threatens-greece-with/

Germany:

https://www.lokalkompass.de/essen-nord/c-politik/respektlos-olaf-scholz_a1623607#gallery=null

https://www.gmx.net/magazine/politik/russland-krieg-ukraine/scholz-sichert-selenskyj-unterstuetzung-38212172

https://www.dw.com/en/schr%C3%B6der-rejects-war-that-will-kill-thousands-in-iraq/a-811719

https://www.news.de/politik/856768712/annalena-baerbock-leitlinien-katalog-fuer-feministische-aussenpolitik-kritik-an-vorschlag-der-gruenen-politikerin-auf-twitter-zerrissen/1/

https://www.spiegel.de/politik/deutschland/bundeswehr-tiger-kampfhub-schrauber-sollen-ersetzt-werden-a-40e6f557-7451-4789-ada4-cc91c7d18a62

USA:

https://newsv2.orf.at/stories/2221556/

https://www.foreignaffairs.com/united-states/robert-kagan-free-world-if-you-can-keep-it-ukraine-america?utm_medium=newsletters&utm_source=twofa&utm_cam-paign=Putin%E2%80%99s%20Last%20Stand&utm_con-tent=20221223&utm_term=FA%20This%20Week%20-%20112017

https://www.foreignaffairs.com/articles/united-states/2021-02-16/super-power-it-or-not
https://www.dailymail.co.uk/news/article-11967397/Leaker-posted-secret-Pentagon-documents-works-military-base-20s.html

https://www.dailymail.co.uk/news/article-11967397/Leaker-posted-secret-Pentagon-documents-works-military-base-20s.html

https://www.wsws.org/en/articles/2023/04/12/pers-a12.pdf

NATO:

https://de.wikipedia.org/wiki/NATO

https://www.nato.int/cps/en/natohq/official_texts_17120.htm?selected-Locale=de
https://www.nato.int/cps/en/natohq/official_texts_17120.htm?selected-Locale=en

https://de.wikipedia.org/wiki/NATO-Gipfel_in_Bukarest_2008

https://natowatch.org/newsbriefs/2018/how-gorbachev-was-misled-over-assurances-against-nato-expansion

https://www.wsws.org/de/articles/2021/11/14/russ-n14.html

https://www.spiegel.de/wirtschaft/kosten-fuer-us-truppen-deutschland-zahlte-fast-eine-milliarde-euro-in-zehn-jahren-a-d4a670c3-8b6f-4b54-8770-eaecf2236d69

https://de.euronews.com/2023/04/20/nato-stoltenberg-kiew-ukraine-selenskyj

Ukraine:

https://de.wikipedia.org/wiki/Kiewer_Rus

https://de.wikipedia.org/wiki/Assoziierungsabkommen_zwischen_der_Europ%C3%A4ischen_Union_und_der_Ukraine

https://de.wikipedia.org/wiki/Orange_Revolution

https://de.wikipedia.org/wiki/Budapester_Memorandum

https://militarywatchmagazine.com/article/western-combatants-flee-ukraine-after-russian-strike-kills-dozens-a-different-kind-of-war-to-iraq-or-afghanistan

https://moderndiplomacy.eu/2023/04/22/ukraine-cant-win-this-war/

https://www.gmx.net/magazine/politik/russland-krieg-ukraine/ukraine-news-26-januar-kampfpanzer-zusage-selenskyj-pocht-militaerhilfe-37757622

https://rmx.news/ukraine/ukraine-is-losing-the-materials-war/?utm_source=newsletter&utm_medium=email&utm_campaign=dutch_farmers_storm_to_victory_german_conservatives_overtake_green_party_and_trash_is_piling_up_in_paris&utm_term=2023-03-19

https://www.gmx.net/magazine/politik/russland-krieg-ukraine/ukraine-news-19-januar-selenskyj-leoparden-liefern-her-37736818

https://www.opensocietyfoundations.org/newsroom/die-open-society-foundations-in-der-ukraine/de

https://www.washingtonpost.com/national-security/2023/04/08/leak-documents-ukraine-air-defense/

https://www.deutschlandfunk.de/newsblog-zum-krieg-in-der-ukraine-150.html

Germany / Russia:

https://www.tagesspiegel.de/politik/absolut-unerwartet-putin-zeigt-sich-enttauscht-von-merkel-wegen-ausserungen-zur-ukraine-9006844.html

https://www.n-tv.de/politik/Baerbock-fliegt-Kriegs-Aussage-um-die-Ohren-article23874295.html

https://www.spiegel.de/politik/annalena-baerbock-reist-als-aussenminis-terin-nach-paris-bruessel-warschau-a-09a8c490-7c6e-4237-82bf-7302e665638a

https://www.rnd.de/politik/ukraine-krieg-wie-reagiert-russland-auf-die-panzer-lieferungen-aus-dem-westen-K65YHG-PZTJHNDETX5HKXN2TDBQ.html?utm_source=pocket-newtab-global-de-DE

Zelenskiy:

https://www.berliner-zeitung.de/wochenende/pandora-papers-volodymyr-selenskij-der-ukrainische-praesident-und-sein-peinliches-net-zwerk-li.188923

https://www.theguardian.com/news/2021/oct/03/revealed-anti-oligarch-ukrainian-president-offshore-connections-volodymyr-zelenskiy

Russia / Ukraine:

https://de.wikipedia.org/wiki/NATO-Russland-Grundakte

https://socialistproject.ca/2019/01/why-does-no-one-care-that-neo-nazis-are-gaining-power-in-ukraine/

https://faridaily.substack.com/p/ukraines-10-point-plan

https://www.bbc.com/news/world-europe-60687203

Nord Stream:

Biden's confession https://www.youtube.com/watch?v=OS4O8rGRLf8

Victoria Nuland and Ted Cruz
https://www.youtube.com/watch?v=VJdbMj8fStA

https://www.spiegel.de/wissenschaft/nord-stream-pipelines-methange-
halt-an-lecks-tausendfach-erhoeht-a-4928880f-d68f-4546-9b5b-69c3be-
b03eb4
[https://www.youtube.com/watch?v=1M0QdAIJSRs

https://www.tichyseinblick.de/daili-es-sentials/linke-wollen-wegen-nord-
stream-die-uno-einschalten/]

https://www.welt.de/politik/ausland/article244301535/Nord-Stream-
Putin-nennt-Beteiligung-von-Ukrainern-an-Anschlaegen-totalen-Unsinn.
html

IVY BELLS

https://www.nytimes.com/1985/11/28/us/ex-security-agency-worrker-is-
said-to-admit-spying-role.html

BALTOPS 22

https://www.navy.mil/Press-Office/News-Stories/Article/3060311/
baltops-22-a-perfect-opportunity-for-research-and-testing-new-techno-
logy/

Poland:

https://foreignpolicy.com/2022/02/23/poland-ukraine-russia-crisis-nato-strategic-role-military-diplomacy-war/

https://www.n-tv.de/politik/Deutschland-leistet-Rekordbeitrag-an-EU-article23811039.html

https://www.firstpost.com/world/poland-considered-partitioning-ukraine-says-former-polish-foreign-minister-12038982.html

https://wiadomosci.radiozet.pl/Gosc-Radia-ZET/radoslaw-sikorski-o-jed-nej-liscie-opozycji-bede-sie-o-to-modlil-23012023

https://www.reuters.com/world/russian-spy-chief-says-us-poland-plot-ting-division-ukraine-2022-04-28/

https://weltwoche.ch/daily/nord-stream-sabotage-polens-praesident-freut-sich-ueber-die-zerstoerung-der-pipelines/

https://www.merkur.de/politik/drohnen-ticker-ukraine-krieg-verhand-lungen-kampfjets-panzer-waffen-lieferung-russland-news-zr-92059289.html?trafficsource=ECRslide

https://www.merkur.de/politik/polen-nato-ukraine-krieg-himars-raketen-stationierung-russland-kaliningrad-kampfjets-92154294.html?traffic-source=ECRslide

https://www.gmx.net/magazine/politik/polen-druck-deutschland-reparationen-erhoehen-37536018

https://rmx.news/poland/we-simply-dont-have-the-ammunition-polish-general-says-poland-can-no-longer-supply-ukraine-with-ammunition-warns-russia-has-resources-to-continue-war/?utm_source=newsletter&utm_medium=email&utm_campaign=inflation_is_hitting_poles_hard_pope_francis_arrives_in_hungary_and_us_air_force_beefs_up_its_presence_in_poland&utm_term=2023-04-28

Lithuania:

https://www.lrt.lt/mediateka/irasas/2000255953/svarbus-pokalbis-landsbergis-lietuva-gali-parodyti-pavyzdi-ir-pirma-nusiusti-kariu-i-ukraina

Russia / USA:

https://www.planet-wissen.de/geschichte/deutsche_geschichte/kalter_krieg/pwiekubakrise100.html

https://www.reuters.com/article/us-shield-poland-russia-idUSLF64954420080815